D1582200

Phil Vickery's
essential
gluten-free

Phil Vickery's
essential
gluten-free

175 RECIPES THAT WILL
REVOLUTIONISE YOUR DIET

WITH BEA HARLING BSc

PHOTOGRAPHY BY KATE WHITAKER

KYLE BOOKS

First published in Great Britain in 2016 by
Kyle Books, an imprint of Kyle Cathie Ltd
192–198 Vauxhall Bridge Road
London SW1V 1DX
general.enquiries@kylebooks.com
www.kylebooks.co.uk

10 9 8 7 6 5 4

ISBN 978 0 85783 284 9

Text © 2016 Phil Vickery
Design © 2016 Kyle Books
Photographs © 2016 Kate Whitaker

Phil Vickery is hereby identified as the
author of this work in accordance with
Section 77 of the Copyright, Designs and
Patents Act 1988.

All rights reserved. No reproduction, copy
or transmission of this publication may
be made without written permission.
No paragraph of this publication may be
reproduced, copied or transmitted save
with written permission or in accordance
with the provisions of the Copyright Act
1956 (as amended). Any person who
does any unauthorised act in relation to
this publication may be liable to criminal
prosecution and civil claims for damages.

EDITOR Judith Hannam
EDITORIAL ASSISTANT Hannah Coughlin
COPY EDITOR Caroline McArthur
DESIGN Ketchup
PHOTOGRAPHER Kate Whitaker
FOOD STYLIST Annie Rigg
HOME ECONOMIST Bea Harling
PROP STYLISTS Lydia Brun and Liz Belton
PRODUCTION Nic Jones and Gemma John

A Cataloguing in Publication record for this
title is available from the British Library.

Colour reproduction by ALTA London
Printed and bound in China by C&C Offset
Printing Co., Ltd.

contents

introduction

In 2008, when I wrote my first GF book, *Seriously Good Gluten-Free Cooking*, it was a foray into the unknown. Most of the other books were about acceptance. I use this word advisedly, because once you were diagnosed with coeliac disease all the things you loved to eat seemed to be off the menu. I remember handing out GF Christmas pudding at a winter show and being struck by the number of people who walked past, waving me away with the words, 'I can't eat that, I'm a coeliac.' When I explained that the puddings were gluten-free, they would stop, pick up the pack and scrutinise the list of ingredients. They would then look at me with narrowed eyes, full of suspicion. Once I had chatted to them and told them that I had the puddings laboratory tested, plus they had the approval of Coeliac UK, they were very happy indeed. It was at this point that I realised there was pretty much nothing out there for coeliacs.

Now, a further two books later (*Seriously Good Gluten-Free Baking* and *Seriously Good Gluten-Free Cooking for Kids*), times have changed – pretty much all for the better. I say pretty much, because there are still a number of people who view coeliac disease as a fad or something you can dip in and out of at will. This is, of course, complete nonsense and makes not only me, but coeliac sufferers too, very angry. One very famous chef once wrote that none of his family or friends was coeliac, but he was a sucker for a 'fad'. It's this kind of ignorance and arrogance that really spurs me on. In fairness, many of the food manufacturers, supermarkets, caterers and restaurant chains have embraced GF, though too often they only pay it lip service. Like most things in life, it comes down to money, and we still have a very long way to go.

A big part of the problem lies in people failing to fully understand the consequences of poisoning a coeliac with gluten. The law now requires chefs to list any of 14 allergens in food being sold to the public. Many complain that this stifles creativity. What rubbish! When I cook, I know exactly what's in my food; to claim otherwise is just laziness.

I have been wanting to write another, larger GF book, one that encompasses the recipes I have found on my travels around the world, for some time. It has taken me the best part of two years and occasionally, if I'm being honest, it has been a bit of a slog. Some days, when unsuccessful versions had to be thrown away it was very frustrating. I always go to great lengths to say that I am no expert. All my books are the result of personal experimentation and playing around trying to get the best out of GF ingredients. One thing I never do is stop learning and testing as more and more ingredients become available. The area that is constantly changing is flour mixes/blends. When I started making my own blends you were pretty much restricted to rice flour, polenta and chickpea flour. Now, buckwheat, soya, brown rice flour and, my current favourite, sorghum, are all readily available. Yes, you could buy one or two commercial mixes, but there are many more now, plus base ingredients such as xanthan gum and tapioca starch that previously you could only ever buy on the internet are now easily obtainable in health shops and supermarkets. Commercial brands will differ from the flour mixes I give in this book, so may not work with the recipes. By all means try them, but be aware that they may need adjusting.

As I have said, this book is the culmination of research from around the world. I have tried to pack in as many recipes as possible, though no doubt have missed out a few favourites. Please read the recipes carefully, especially when it comes to baking, cakes, puds, flours, etc. Weighing ingredients correctly on a set of good scales is essential to GF cooking. Calibrating your oven is another essential. No one ever gets them tested; we all assume the temperature controls are correct! Some recipes even work better when the fan setting is not on, using top and bottom heat only.

I really hope you and your family enjoy the book and, rest assured, I will continue to bang the drum harder than ever for coeliacs worldwide. **Phil Vickery**

What is coeliac disease?

Coeliac disease is frequently and widely misunderstood. Often regarded as an allergy or simple food intolerance, it is in fact a lifelong, autoimmune disease affecting the gut and other parts of the body. It is caused by an inflammatory response to gluten, a protein found in wheat, barley and rye. Some people are also affected by oats. Gluten, a collective name for the type of protein found in these cereals, is what gives bread its elasticity and cakes their spring and, unfortunately, even the tiniest amount can cause problems for those with coeliac disease. The small intestine is lined with small, finger-like projections called villi. These play a crucial role in digestion as they increase the surface area of the small intestine and allow essential nutrients to be absorbed into the bloodstream. However, for people with coeliac disease, when gluten comes into contact with the villi, it triggers a response by the immune system which attacks the villi, as if it were a 'foreign' substance. The villi very quickly become damaged and inflamed and incapable of extracting key nutrients from the food we eat.

What are the symptoms?

The malabsorption described above quickly leads to cramps, gas, bloating, flatulence and diarrhoea. It is quite common for these to be put down to irritable bowel syndrome (IBS), and only later to be recognised as coeliac disease.

Diarrhoea is certainly common and yet it is important to note that sufferers can present many and varied symptoms; some may have a normal bowel habit or even tend towards constipation, children may not gain weight or grow properly, while adults may find they lose weight. Malabsorption may also leave people tired and weak, because of anaemia caused by iron or folate deficiency.

In fact, rather than experiencing bowel problems, many coeliac sufferers approach their doctor because of extreme tiredness and psychological problems such as depression. There can also be a calcium deficiency due to malabsorption, resulting in low bone density and sometimes even fractures (as a result of osteoporosis). Bone and muscle pain can also be a problem, as can ulcers in the mouth or a blistering, itchy skin rash mostly on the elbows and knees (called dermatitis herpetiformis).

Typical symptoms

Diarrhoea, fatigue and iron deficiency stem directly from the malabsorption of nutrients, but there is a range of other symptoms, including:

- Bloating
- Abdominal pains
- Nausea
- Weight loss (but not in all cases)
- Mouth ulcers
- Hair loss
- Skin rash
- Defective tooth enamel
- Nerve problems

How do I get diagnosed?

If you suspect you may suffer from coeliac disease, don't panic. Just remember, it is entirely manageable with a controlled diet. In fact, if you are one of the many, many undiagnosed sufferers, you'll probably be pleased to find out that you really do have a condition and, better yet, that there is a course of action to alleviate the symptoms.

The first thing to do is talk to your doctor, as they will be able to perform a simple blood test. It is important to follow your normal diet leading up to the test as confirmation is provided by the presence of antibodies in the blood which have been triggered by a coeliac's response to gluten. To obtain an accurate test result it is necessary to consume food that contains gluten every day for a minimum of six weeks, as following a gluten-free diet for even a few days slows down your immune systems antibody production to 'normal' levels and the test will give a false negative.

If the test is positive, it is recommended you then have an intestinal biopsy, which examines the villi in the small intestine under a microscope to check for damage. This will provide you with confirmation of your diagnosis before you embark on a lifelong diet of gluten avoidance. This biopsy must also be done after a gluten-based diet for accurate diagnosis. However, children may not always need a biopsy when being tested as if they have symptoms of coeliac disease and a blood test that shows high levels of antibodies, a second antibody blood test followed by a genetic test can be used to confirm the diagnosis.

What is the treatment?

Treatment is a gluten-free diet, which means that wheat, barley, rye and their derivatives must all be avoided. Most people are able to tolerate uncontaminated oats, although some need to avoid them. Strict adherence to the diet allows the intestines to heal, leading to resolution of symptoms and reducing the risk of complications like osteoporosis.

What can I eat?

There are many naturally gluten-free foods, including potatoes, rice and maize, all fresh meat, poultry and fish, all fresh fruit and vegetables, fresh herbs, spices, dried pulses, rice noodles, plain nuts, eggs, dairy products, sugar, honey, pure oils and vinegars, vanilla extract and fresh yeast. Coeliac UK has a useful Gluten-free Checklist which can be accessed at www.coeliac.org.uk/GlutenFreeChecklist. The Charity also produces information on thousands of products you can eat.

Foods that are naturally gluten-free

- all fresh meat and fish
- all fresh fruit and vegetables
- fresh herbs and individual spices
- corn and cornmeal (maize/sweetcorn)
- dried peas, lentils, pulses and beans
- rice and wild rice
- rice bran
- plain nuts and seeds
- eggs
- dairy products – milk, cream, natural yogurt, cheese
- soya and plain tofu
- sugar
- honey
- golden syrup
- maple syrup
- treacle
- jams and marmalade
- pure oils and fats
- vinegars
- tomato purée
- vanilla essence and extract
- fresh yeast

What about contamination?

Even the tiniest amount of gluten can make someone with coeliac disease ill. Dry gluten-containing ingredients like flour and breadcrumbs are high risk for contamination when you are producing gluten-free meals. It is a good idea to keep gluten-free food and ingredients separate from gluten-containing foods. Tips for avoiding contamination in the kitchen include:

- cleaning surfaces immediately before their use
- using clean frying oil for chips and gluten-free foods
- NOT reusing oil for breaded or battered products foods
- keeping all pans, utensils and colanders separate during food preparation and cooking
- using a clean grill, separate toaster or toaster bags
- making sure that butter or spreads are not contaminated with breadcrumbs

Foods and drinks that may include gluten without you realising it

- baking powder
- communion wafers
- 'corn tortillas' may also contain regular flour
- frozen chips – these may be coated with flour
- stock cubes/powder
- vegetable soup may contain pearl barley
- seasoning mixes
- mustard products
- packet suet may have flour in it to stop it sticking together
- commercial salad dressings and mayonnaise
- soy sauce (there are gluten-free brands available)
- dry-roasted nuts
- pretzels
- Bombay mix
- Scotch eggs
- food that has been deep-fried with other gluten-containing food, e.g. battered fish and chips
- flavoured crisps
- malted milk drinks
- barley water or flavoured barley water
- beer, lager, stout and ale

Gluten-free alternatives

There are a number of naturally gluten-free flours that are becoming more widely available. It is important to check the packaging though, as some can become contaminated with gluten during the milling process.

- rice flour
- tapioca/cassava flour
- potato flour
- cornflour
- cornmeal (polenta)
- soya flour
- gram/chickpea flour
- chestnut flour
- buckwheat flour
- lotus root flour
- carob flour
- millet flour
- quinoa flour
- sorghum
- arrowroot
- linseed
- sago
- teff

Food labels

By law, manufacturers have to list all the ingredients in food products. In addition, allergens, including gluten-containing cereals, must be emphasised in the ingredients, for example in bold lettering. When shopping and cooking, always check the label to make sure you choose a suitable product.

COELIAC UK

Coeliac UK is the leading charity working for people with coeliac disease and dermatitis herpetiformis (DH). Their mission is to improve the lives of people living with the condition through information, support, campaigning and research. Their vision is that the needs of people with coeliac disease and DH are universally recognised and met.

Coeliac UK offers a range of support services, providing expert and independent information to help people with coeliac disease manage their health and diet. They produce a comprehensive range of information booklets, leaflets and publications. The Helpline and the website, featuring a special Members Only Area, provide additional news, information and advice. They also have a smartphone app, Gluten-free on the Move, to help you shop for gluten-free items, and it even includes a handy scanner so you can scan items as you shop.

Members are a vital part of Coeliac UK's work as campaigners, fundraisers and volunteers. There are many ways people can get involved with Coeliac UK, including helping to raise awareness and improve life for people who are living life gluten-free.

If you are diagnosed with coeliac disease or dermatitis herpetiformis and would like to become a Member of Coeliac UK, or if you think that you or a family member may have coeliac disease, please call 0333 332 2033 or visit their website at www.coeliac.org.uk.

flours, pancakes,
breads & pastries

gluten-free flour blends

Making a blend of different flours allows you to add personality, texture and flavour to a recipe, as no single grain or seed flour will perform quite like wheat flour. However, once you know a little about each alternative flour and its character, it will give you the confidence to experiment. Although alternative flours are naturally gluten-free, some can become contaminated with gluten during the milling process. Make sure you check the labels.

All-purpose gluten-free flours

Gluten-free flour blends are readily available and generally work well as store cupboard standbys. Some, including the self-raising version, contain fixed amounts of raising agents, as well as xanthan gum, which improves the texture, making cakes, for example, less crumbly. If you make your own blends, however, you can control the proportions of these ingredients and have a selection of mixtures rather than one all-purpose flour for everything. Other all-purpose flour mixes, including some from the USA, contain ingredients, such as bicarbonate of soda and GF baking powder. If you use these you could find yourself with unexpected results.

Substituting gluten-free flours into a standard recipe

Gluten-free flours tend to be more absorbent, so if doing this you will probably need to increase the amount of liquid. Expect the baking time, texture and rise all to be slightly different. Add a small amount of xanthan gum with the flour to replicate the stretchy 'spring' and structure: ½ teaspoon to 225g of flour as a general guide. It is a fine balance; too little and the structure will fall apart; too much and your cake will bounce like a ball. Don't forget to make a note of what you did so you can do the same (or avoid doing the same) again.

BAKING POWDER

This is a leavening agent that will help your baking recipes to rise. Shop bought baking powder usually contains gluten, so you need to check for a suitable product or make your own. To do this, mix together 2 parts cream of tartar with 1 part bicarbonate of soda (also called baking soda). For example, 2 teaspoons of cream of tartar with 1 teaspoon of bicarbonate of soda. The amount you need depends on the type of recipe, so it's difficult to be precise, but, as a rule of thumb, add 2 level teaspoons of GF baking powder to 225g of plain flour blend, for example: 2 level teaspoons of GF baking powder per 225g flour for a sponge cake, 1 level teaspoon of GF baking powder per 225g of flour for batter and 1 level teaspoon of GF baking powder for biscuits and pastry.

Blending your own flour

Mix all combinations of flours together very thoroughly and evenly. If you add xanthan gum (or baking powder) to a recipe, make sure you sift it with the flour a couple of times, to mix it well and avoid an uneven rise or texture.

THE BASE

Start with heavier flours such as sorghum (jowar), brown rice, white rice (only use a little), maize and cornmeal (polenta) flour. A mixture of these contains more protein and fibre than white rice flour and is closer to baking with wholewheat flour. They tend to give a denser, darker and less risen result. Look for fine-milled versions rather than those with a coarse-grain texture.

THE BODY

Next, you need to blend the base with some airier starches to lighten the body of the flour and tone down the more characterful base notes. Tapioca starch (made from cassava root) contributes much to a good crumb texture and helps bind the batter or dough. At a pinch, you can use cornflour if you cannot find tapioca, but tapioca lends a certain 'chew' to the structure and you may notice when it's not there. Starchy flours like cornflour, arrowroot and potato starch (not potato flour) all help towards a light, soft structure.

TAPIOCA

SWEET WHITE
SORGHUM FLOUR

CORNMEAL

CORNFLOUR

RICE FLOUR

MAIZE MEAL

POTATO FLOUR

Depending on the recipe, you can add some personality and attitude – ingredients with big, bold flavours or a nutritional boost – opening up a world of more interesting and healthier recipes than using wheat flour alone can provide. They are best added for an individual recipe, rather than in your basic blend, however.

Here you can play with a huge variety of ingredients: buckwheat (a relative of rhubarb), millet, teff, soy, chickpea (or gram) flours and quinoa, flax meal, rice bran (for added fibre), almond and nut flours or coconut flour. Use little and sparingly: although nutritious, they have a strong flavour you may dislike if allowed to dominate the flour blend, though a touch more vanilla in a recipe can help to soften them. White rice flour generally gives a gritty or sandy mouthfeel, while bean flours can taste bitter, with an off-putting smell. You might also find yourself balancing the cost of these ingredients, as some can be expensive. Refer to the glossary (pages 250–252) for more detailed descriptions and tips.

Texture and flavour

CREATING SUBTLE TEXTURES AND FLAVOURS

For a smoother or fluffy, close texture, add specialist flours such as almond or chestnut flour. Replace 10 per cent of the flour blend to change the character of the recipe.

When baking with gluten-free ingredients, a dry or crumbly texture is common. The following offer some solutions:

- Using oil instead of solid fats makes a light, moist and less crumbly sponge.
- Adding yogurt or crème fraîche to some cake, scone and muffin mixtures adds moisture, and gives a smoother texture.
- Additions such as apple, dates, banana, carrot, beetroot, grated courgette, etc. tend to hold the structure together where gluten is lacking. The result is delicious and moist.
- With all of these suggestions, don't make a straight swap without trying one of the recipes included in the book first.

Boosting nutrient content

Substituting 10 per cent of your blend with high-protein flours such as teff, buckwheat, amaranth, sorghum or quinoa can improve nutrient content. However, all are bold-flavoured and some are slightly bitter, so use sparingly. Coconut flour helps lower the glycaemic index, but is very thirsty. Flaxseed and chia flours are sources of omega 3, and have gelling properties that make them a good substitute for xanthan gum (ground flaxseed can also sometimes replace egg), but both can affect texture and dramatically alter the amount of liquid needed. All three contain high amounts of fibre, which tends to be more slowly digested and better for gut health. Bottom line: include this group of interesting ingredients in very small proportions.

Storing gluten-free flours

Gluten-free flours can be expensive and have a short shelf life, so store in a cool, dry and dark area for best results.

Choosing gluten-free flours

There are a number of naturally gluten-free flours that are becoming more widely available. While these are made from naturally gluten-free ingredients, it is important to check the packaging as some can become contaminated with gluten during the milling process. The flours listed in this section are naturally gluten-free but we have marked them as GF so you know to check the label in case of cross contamination. When choosing your flours, make sure they are either marked as gluten-free or that they do not have an advisory statement to say that they might be contaminated.

GF polenta flour blend

Makes 500g

Good for muffins and chocolate cakes, this adds texture. If you prefer, use gluten-free chestnut flour instead of polenta.

150g (30 per cent) very fine-milled GF polenta or fine maize flour
250g (50 per cent) GF sorghum flour
100g (20 per cent) GF tapioca flour

Sift all the flours together very thoroughly and evenly, or put into a food-processor and pulse until mixed. Store in an airtight container.

GF sorghum flour blend

Makes 500g

I use a sorghum flour blend wherever possible because I like its flavour and higher protein and fibre content. Sorghum flour can be used in preference to (or blended with) brown rice flour for a finer texture. It is soft, slightly sweet and gives good results when combined with millet and oat flours for an alternative gluten-free blend.

A wholegrain, milled to light tan-coloured flour, sorghum isn't suitable for delicate paler cakes, but is good for muffins, cookies, fruitcakes and other bakes where a lighter colour and flavour are not critical. It is also good for when you would use a light wholemeal type of flour.

175g (35 per cent) GF sorghum flour
175g (35 per cent) potato starch
150g (30 per cent) GF tapioca flour

Sift all the flours together very thoroughly and evenly, or put into a food-processor and pulse until well mixed. Store in an airtight container.

GF white bread flour blend

Quantity for 1 x 400g loaf, or 8–10 bread rolls

Good for everyday 'white bread'-style loaves, rolls or pizza bases.

70g (17.5 per cent) GF brown rice flour
70g (17.5 per cent) GF white rice flour
140g (35 per cent) potato starch
60g (15 per cent) GF tapioca flour/starch
60g (15 per cent) cornflour

Quantity for a 250g pizza base
90g (36 per cent) GF rice flour, half white and half brown
80g (32 per cent) potato starch
40g (40 per cent) GF tapioca flour/starch
40g (40 per cent) cornflour

Sift the flours together very thoroughly and evenly, or put into a food-processor and pulse until mixed. Store in an airtight container.

GF white and brown rice flour blend

Makes 500g

Good for when a lighter colour and more delicate flavour are needed. Use very fine-milled rice flour to avoid a gritty result.

175g (35 per cent) GF rice flour, half white and half brown
175g (35 per cent) potato starch
150g (30 per cent) GF tapioca flour/starch

Sift together very thoroughly or put into a food-processor and pulse until mixed. Store in an airtight container.

GF flour mix A

Makes 1kg

The following recipes are the original gluten-free flour blends from my earlier books and are good basic blends to cook with.

700g (70 per cent) GF fine white rice flour
200g (20 per cent) GF potato starch
100g (10 per cent) GF tapioca flour/starch

Sift the flours together very thoroughly and evenly, or put into a food-processor and pulse until mixed. Store in an airtight container.

GF flour mix B

Makes 1kg

500g (50 per cent) GF brown rice flour
300g (30 per cent) fine maize meal
200g (20 per cent) cornflour

Sift the flours together very thoroughly and evenly, or put into a food-processor and pulse until mixed. Store in an airtight container.

top tips for gluten-free baking

When baking with gluten-free alternatives it's usually best to follow your instincts – the batch of flour, temperature and humidity on the day, and other foibles, will all make the results vary. Many challenges can result from the lack of 'glue' and stretch you get from the gluten in wheat. A number of gluten-free flours can also give dry results. To overcome a dry texture when making cakes, baking with vegetable oil helps make the crumb softer and moister. Ground almonds, seeds, roasted vegetables and fruit are all helpful too. Gluten-free cakes may be more crumbly: in this case, eggs, ground flaxseed and xanthan gum all help.

Other things I have found to help include:

• When baking with gluten-free ingredients follow the instructions carefully. Be accurate with measurements and temperatures. Weigh carefully and mix thoroughly.

• Use the correct tin size because it affects the cooking time and texture.

• Out-of-date ingredients can give poor results. Replace gluten-free baking powder every 6–9 months.

• For best results, start with all the ingredients at room temperature and have them all ready to begin with. Use a light touch when mixing as overbeating can cause the batter to seize.

• After mixing, gluten-free batters can look and behave a little differently to wheat-based flour mixtures. Generally, gluten-free batters are wetter and thinner, but there are many exceptions to catch you out: for example, chocolate mixtures, especially with cocoa powder, can be thicker.

• Mixtures tend to stiffen when standing and soak up the moisture even more. Be sure to mix and bake straight away, especially if using baking powder or xanthan gum.

• Too much mixture in the tin can cause a cake to sink in the middle. Too much baking powder and a mixture that is too wet can also have the same effect.

• The amount of liquid needed often differs with the ingredients and type of flour you use, or even between batches of the same flour, so learn to judge and adjust to the description in the recipe. Egg sizes also vary and will affect this too.

• Too little liquid and the result can be heavy and dry. You will need to increase the liquid if you are substituting gluten-free flour into a normal recipe.

• However, the type of flour you use will also influence how much more liquid you need to add; coconut flour, for example, is very thirsty, and all flours grab moisture from a humid day.

• Your oven will have its own personality, so get to know it (and your microwave) and adjust cooking times and temperatures to suit your individual oven. You might find an oven thermometer useful because variation in oven performance is a big cause of baking disappointment. Preheat the oven, use the centre shelf and don't be tempted to open the oven door to peek until at least three-quarters of the way through the baking time. Keep a sharp eye on what's in the oven until you get used to cooking gluten free.

• When using a fan oven, refer to the manufacturer's handbook for the correct oven temperature adjustment: usually 10–20°C lower than conventional, although please note that lower temperatures can stay the same.

• Often, baking slower, at lower temperatures, is sound baking practice. If your oven regularly turns out results that are under baked, adjust the temperature up and vice versa.

• Gluten-free baked goods do not keep well; they are best eaten fresh, or frozen when cool and defrosted as you need them. When defrosted, they will come back to just-baked freshness if popped in a microwave for a few seconds before eating.

For more information see Gluten-free Flours (pages 14–15).

lining a pastry case

It's easier to roll the dough between two sheets of cling film or baking parchment. You may also find it easier if the dough is cold, but not rock hard, and rested. If rolling directly on the work surface, sprinkle it, and the rolling pin, with gluten-free flour. Because the pastry is so fragile, I use a whole egg to glaze and set three times for extra stability and to stop the pastry going soggy.

---

1 quantity of your chosen pastry dough (such as Classic Shortcrust Pastry, page 40)
1 egg, beaten

1. Roll the pastry until it's about 5cm larger than the size of the tart tin, if using, so that there's enough pastry to leave an overhang, or roll to the thickness you want.

2. Peel off the top layer of cling film. Flour the surface of the pastry and the rolling pin, and gently roll the pastry around the rolling pin. Lift it over the tin and carefully unroll the pastry over the top. Use a small ball of dough to lightly press the pastry into the shape of the tin. Press the edges down gently to reinforce them and then trim the top.

3. Line the pastry case with a layer of thin, slightly scrunched baking parchment, carefully pushing it into the edges and up the sides (scrunching the paper makes it more pliable and less likely to push though the pastry). This will help the sides to stay up where you have shaped them.

4. Half-fill the tart with ceramic baking beans or dried pulses (although I have cooked many a blind-baked case without paper and beans and it does work very well; try it). Chill or freeze the pastry case while you preheat the oven to 190°C/180°C fan/gas mark 5.

5. Bake for about 15 minutes until the pastry is firm. Remove the paper lining and beans, if using, and brush the case with the beaten egg. Return the empty case to the oven and bake for a few more minutes, until the egg is just set. Repeat this three times, coating with egg and returning to the oven to set each time.

6. When cool enough to handle, balance the tin on a can or jar and gently ease down the sides.

buckwheat pancakes

Gluten-free, thin buckwheat pancakes are easy to make; just add your favourite sweet toppings or fill with something savoury. You can replace the milk with dairy and lactose free versions. If you use a different flour blend, check that it doesn't have a raising agent or xanthan gum added and, as always with gluten-free flours, you may need to adjust the quantity of liquid to get the right consistency.

40g GF brown rice flour
40g GF white rice flour
20g potato starch
20g GF tapioca flour/starch
1 tablespoon GF buckwheat
 flour
¼ level teaspoon xanthan gum
½ teaspoon salt
1 medium egg
200–225ml milk
25g butter, or dairy-free
 baking spread, melted
oil, for greasing
lemon juice and a sprinkling
 of sugar, to serve (optional)

Makes 6 x 8cm pancakes · **PREP TIME** *15 minutes* · **COOKING TIME** *20 minutes*

1. In a bowl, combine the flours, xanthan gum and salt.

2. Add the egg and gradually whisk in the milk to give a thickish, smooth batter the consistency of pouring double cream. Add a touch more or less liquid to get the right thickness. Stir in the melted butter.

3. Grease a non-stick frying pan with a little oil and heat until hot. Spoon some batter into the pan and quickly swirl and spread the batter thinly to an 8cm circle.

4. Cook the pancake on one side until bubbles appear, then flip it over and cook the other side. Transfer to a plate and stack between sheets of greaseproof paper to keep warm while you cook the rest of the pancakes.

5. Serve with a squeeze of lemon juice and a sprinkling of sugar, or your favourites, like ground cinnamon, maple syrup or savoury fillings.

buttermilk pancakes

These are thick American-style pancakes to have with bacon and maple syrup for a weekend breakfast treat. Or, rather than adding a topping, try stirring 100g of berries, such as blueberries, blackberries or blackcurrants, into the pancake batter before cooking.

Try this pancake mix with the buckwheat, but you can just leave it out. If you use a different flour blend, check if it already has a raising agent. If so, you may need to adjust the liquid for the right consistency.

40g GF brown rice flour
40g GF white rice flour
20g potato starch
20g GF tapioca flour/starch
1 tablespoon GF buckwheat
   flour (optional)
1 teaspoon GF baking powder
a pinch of salt
1 medium egg
200g buttermilk or thin yogurt
1–2 tablespoons milk
25g unsalted butter, melted
oil, for greasing
maple syrup and grilled bacon,
   to serve

Makes about 8 x 8cm pancakes · **PREP TIME** *15 minutes* · **COOKING TIME** *20 minutes*

1. In a bowl, combine the flours, baking powder and salt.

2. Add the egg and gradually whisk in the buttermilk or yogurt, and enough milk to give a thick, smooth batter the consistency of loosely whipped double cream. Whisk in the melted butter.

3. Grease a non-stick frying pan with a little oil and heat until hot. Spoon some batter into the pan and quickly swirl and spread the batter thinly to an 8-cm circle.

4. Cook the pancake on one side until bubbles appear, then flip it over and cook the other side. Transfer to a plate and stack between sheets of greaseproof paper to keep warm while you cook the rest of the pancakes.

5. Serve with maple syrup and bacon.

waffles

I use a waffle iron purpose-built for the job, but if you do not have one you can use small blini pans or even a large frying pan, and spoon in the mix a bit like you would do for drop scones.

2 medium eggs
2 tablespoons vegetable oil
125ml buttermilk or
   thin yogurt
175ml milk
250g GF rice flour, half
   brown and half white
a pinch of salt
½ teaspoon GF baking powder
½ teaspoon bicarbonate
   of soda
oil, for greasing

Makes 4 · **PREP TIME** *5 minutes* · **COOKING TIME** *15 minutes*

1. Oil and preheat the waffle maker, or heat a blini pan or frying pan over a high heat.

2. In a bowl, whisk together the eggs, oil, buttermilk and milk.

3. In a separate bowl, mix together the rice flours, salt, baking powder and bicarbonate of soda, then whisk the dry ingredients into the wet until you have a smooth, thickish batter.

4. Spread one-quarter of the batter into the base of the hot waffle iron and cook for about 3 minutes, depending on your waffle iron. Alternatively, spoon a quarter of the mixture onto the base of the hot pan and try to keep a neat shape. Flip once the bottom is cooked. Repeat with the remaining mixture.

5. When the waffles are done, place them in a warm oven until you are ready to eat.

gluten-free bread

This is an all-round everyday loaf; great for sandwiches or toast. For a dairy-free version, just use water instead of the milk.

400g GF White Bread Flour
   Blend (page 15), plus extra
   for dusting
2 level teaspoons xanthan gum
1 teaspoon salt
1 tablespoon caster sugar
7g GF fast-action dried yeast
150ml warm milk
150ml warm water
1 medium egg, at room
   temperature
2 teaspoons cider vinegar
3 tablespoons olive oil, plus
   2 teaspoons
2 teaspoons mixed seeds such
   as flax, sunflower or poppy,
   for sprinkling

Makes 1 medium loaf · **PREP TIME** *15 minutes, plus proving* · **COOKING TIME** *45 minutes*

1. Preheat the oven to 200°C/190°C fan/gas mark 6. Oil a 900g loaf tin and dust with flour.

2. In a bowl, mix together the flour, xanthan gum, salt, sugar and yeast well so that they are evenly combined to avoid uneven rising.

3. Pour the warm milk and water into a jug then pour three-quarters of it (225ml) into a large bowl if you're using a hand mixer, or the bowl of a stand mixer and add the egg, vinegar and the 3 tablespoons of olive oil.

4. Tip in the flour mixture and beat on low to start, then on high for about 3 minutes to form a soft, smooth and sticky dough. It will resemble a thick cake mixture more than a bread dough and will drop slowly from the beater. If it seems a little dry, add more of the water/milk mixture.

5. Scrape the dough into the oiled and floured loaf tin, spread it with a spatula and smooth the top. Dot the top with the 2 teaspoons of olive oil, then wet your fingers and press the seeds over the top.

6. Leave the loaf in a warm place for about 20 minutes or so to rise just up to the rim of the tin; no more or it won't be able to hold its shape.

7. Bake for 40–45 minutes until nicely browned on the top and sides. Remove the loaf from the tin to test if it is baked; if you tap the bottom it should sound 'hollow'. Now try to resist cutting a slice until it has cooled.

TIP *You won't have to knead gluten-free dough; the consistency is more like cake batter. In theory, there's no need to prove it either, but I find it makes this loaf lighter. If it's difficult to find a warm place, try preheating the oven to 50°C (an oven thermometer will help here). Oil the top of the dough and place it on a baking tray. Put a couple of upturned mugs either side of the tin and lay cling film over the top (the mugs will keep it from sticking to the dough). Put the baking tray in the oven, turn off the heat and leave the dough to prove until it reaches just below the rim of the tin. Remove the cling film and cups, turn up the heat to 200°C and bake. It won't take long for the dough to rise, so keep an eye on it; if you prove it for too long it will be in danger of sinking like a crater.*

everyday bread maker loaf

This is similar to the recipe opposite, but made in a bread maker. It is worth using a variety of flours here to achieve a good texture. For a dairy-free version, just use water instead of the milk.

400g GF White Bread Flour Blend (page 15), plus extra for dusting

150ml warm milk

150ml warm water

2 medium eggs, at room temperature

2 teaspoons cider vinegar

3 tablespoons olive oil

2 level teaspoons xanthan gum

1 teaspoon salt

1 tablespoon caster sugar

7g GF fast-action dried yeast

2 teaspoons mixed seeds such as flax, sunflower or poppy, for sprinkling

Makes 1 medium loaf · **PREP TIME** *5 minutes* · **COOKING TIME** *2 hours*

1. Oil a 900g loaf tin and dust with flour.

2. Pour the warm milk and water, eggs, vinegar and oil into the pan of the bread maker.

3. In a separate bowl, measure the flours, xanthan gum, salt, sugar and yeast, then mix well so they are evenly combined.

4. Tip the flour mixture into the pan on top of the liquid. Start the programme on a gluten-free setting or basic programme. After a couple of minutes, scrape down the dough from the sides of the pan with a plastic spatula.

5. When the machine has finished beating, add the seeds for the top if your bread maker has a separate feature to enable this. Otherwise add them after the mixing stage or in with the dry ingredients. Leave the bread maker to do its thing and don't worry if the seeds get mixed in.

6. Once baked, leave the bread to cool in the machine for 10 minutes, then turn it out of the pan onto a cooling rack.

NOTE *If you use a ready-made commercial flour it may already have xanthan gum added, so you won't need more; different flours also require different quantities of liquid, so remember to adjust the recipe to get the right texture.*

TRY THIS *Either recipe could be made into a wholemeal-style loaf by using 300g of the bread flour blend and swapping the remaining 100g with a mixture of wholegrain flours such as sorghum, buckwheat, amaranth or teff. You can mix more seeds into the dough before proving if you like. Try linseed, millet, poppy, sunflower and sesame seeds.*

multiseed bread rolls

These soft rolls are egg free and dairy free, with a nice open texture. They look good with a sprinkling of seeds on top and are delicious served warm. As with all gluten-free breads, these are best eaten fresh or stored in the freezer to be warmed up as and when you need them. Using mini loaf cases or tins provides the necessary structure to hold and shape the dough; if you haven't got mini loaf-shaped tins you can use an oiled and dusted muffin tin instead.

400g GF White Bread Flour Blend (page 15), plus extra for dusting, or use the quantities below:

70g GF brown rice flour

70g GF white rice flour

140g potato starch

60g GF tapioca flour/starch

60g cornflour

1 level teaspoon xanthan gum

1 teaspoon salt

2 teaspoons caster sugar

7g GF fast-action dried yeast

250–300ml warm water

1 teaspoon cider vinegar

1 teaspoon olive oil

50g mixed seeds such as linseed, flax, sunflower, poppy, millet or sesame

Makes 8 mini loaves • **PREP TIME** *15 minutes, plus proving* • **COOKING TIME** *20 minutes*

1. Lightly oil and dust with flour eight 6 x 8cm mini loaf tins. Cut strips of baking parchment to line each tin, with enough parchment at either end to make handles for easing out the baked rolls.

2. In a bowl, measure the flour, xanthan gum, salt, sugar and yeast, and mix well so that they are evenly combined.

3. Pour 250ml of the warm water, the vinegar and oil into a large bowl if you're using a hand mixer, or the bowl of a stand mixer. Tip the flour mixture in and beat on low to start, then on high for about 3 minutes to form a soft, smooth and sticky dough. It will be more like a thick cake mixture than a bread dough and will drop slowly from the beater. If it seems a little dry, add a touch more water.

4. Beat the mixed seeds into the dough, reserving a few for the top.

5. Spoon the dough into the oiled and dusted loaf tins so that they are about half full and spread using the back of a wet spoon or fingers to smooth the top. Score the tops lengthways using a sharp knife. Sprinkle a few seeds over and press them lightly into the dough. Set aside while you preheat the oven to 220°C/200°C fan/gas mark 6.

6. Bake for about 20 minutes until nicely browned on top: if you take one of the rolls out of the tin and tap the bottom it should sound 'hollow'.

soft milk bread rolls

This dough is too soft to shape on a tray so they are baked
in a muffin tin.

400g GF White Bread Flour
Blend (page 15), plus extra
for dusting, or use the
quantities below:
70g GF brown rice flour
70g GF white rice flour
140g potato starch
60g GF tapioca flour/starch
60g cornflour

2 level teaspoons xanthan gum
1 teaspoon salt
1 tablespoon caster sugar
7g GF fast-action dried yeast
150ml warm milk
150ml warm water
2 medium eggs, at room
temperature
2 teaspoons cider vinegar
3 tablespoons olive oil
2 teaspoons olive oil,
for glazing

Makes 12 rolls • **PREP TIME** *15 minutes, plus proving* • **COOKING TIME** *20 minutes*

1. Lightly oil and flour a 12-hole muffin tin. If using mini loaf tins, the dough makes 8–10, depending on the size of the loaf tins used (see tip below).

2. In a bowl, measure the flour, xanthan gum, salt, sugar and yeast, and mix well until evenly combined.

3. Add the warm milk, water, eggs, vinegar and the 3 tablespoons of olive oil to a large bowl if you're using a hand mixer, or the bowl of a stand mixer.

4. Tip the flour mixture into the bowl and beat on low to start then on high for about 3 minutes to form a soft, smooth and sticky dough. It will resemble a thick cake mixture more than a bread dough and will drop slowly from the beater. If it seems a little dry, add a touch more water.

5. Divide the dough between the muffin holes and spread using the back of a wet spoon or fingers to smooth the tops. The holes should be about two-thirds full, with about 100g of dough in each one. Score the tops and coat them with the 2 teaspoons of olive oil and set aside while you preheat the oven to 220°C/200°C fan/gas mark 6.

6. Bake for about 20 minutes until nicely browned on top. If you take one of the rolls out of the tin and tap the bottom it should sound 'hollow'.

NOTE *If you use a ready-made commercial flour it may already have xanthan gum added, so you won't need more; different flours also require different quantities of liquid, so remember to adjust the recipe to get the right texture.*

TIP *You can use mini loaf tins to shape the dough for the rolls. They look good with a small slash on top and you can serve them warm still in their paper cases, if using.*

soft brioche

Buttery brioche is one of life's great pleasures. The longer the dough is left to prove the better, so the best thing to do is to leave it overnight.

75ml warm water

125ml warm milk

1 large egg, at room temperature

250g GF fine white rice flour

50g GF potato flour

25g GF tapioca flour/starch

2 level teaspoons xanthan gum

1 teaspoon salt

25g caster sugar

7g GF fast-action dried yeast

200g cold unsalted butter, cut into cubes

Makes 1 medium loaf · **PREP TIME** *15 minutes, plus proving overnight* · **COOKING TIME** *25–30 minutes*

1. Pour the warm water and milk into a jug, add the egg and beat lightly.

2. Put the flours, xanthan gum, salt, sugar and yeast into a food processor and pulse to mix. Add the butter and process briefly to cut the butter into the mixture. Don't mix the butter in completely; you want to leave some very small pieces in the mixture.

3. Tip into a large bowl, make a well in the centre and add the milk and egg mixture. Fold the ingredients together briefly; the mixture will still be a bit lumpy.

4. Cover the bowl with cling film and leave to prove in the fridge overnight.

5. Preheat the oven to 220°C/200°C fan/gas mark 7. Oil a 900g loaf tin and spoon the proved mixture into the tin.

6. Bake for 25–30 minutes, or until well-risen and dark golden. Remove from the oven and eat warm.

soda bread

This is a simple and fast bread to make fresh for breakfast. The bicarbonate of soda is activated by the acidity of the buttermilk. If you like you can add mixed seeds, chopped fresh herbs or olives, sundried tomatoes, dried fruit or chorizo. You can also make it without the oat flour; just make it up to 250g flour in total.

175g GF Sorghum Flour
    Blend (page 15), plus
    extra for dusting
75g GF oat flour
1 level teaspoon xanthan gum
1½ level teaspoons
    bicarbonate of soda
½ teaspoon salt
1 teaspoon light soft
    brown sugar
200ml buttermilk
about 75ml milk
2 teaspoons GF rolled oats
    for the top, or a dusting
    of GF wholegrain flour

TIP *You can also substitute gluten- and wheat-free beer for the 75ml milk for a nice change.*

Makes 1 small loaf · **PREP TIME** *15 minutes* · **COOKING TIME** *40 minutes*

1. Preheat the oven to 220°C/200°C fan/gas mark 7. Line a baking tray with baking parchment and dust liberally with flour.

2. In a large bowl, measure the flours, xanthan gum, bicarbonate of soda, salt and sugar, and mix well so they are evenly combined.

3. Pour the buttermilk over the dry ingredients and stir in enough milk to form a thick, sticky dough.

4. Tip the dough out onto the floured baking parchment; it will still break and crumble. Coat your hands in flour if the dough is sticky, and lift the dough and turn it to shape it into a ball, rather than kneading it. This will help to give the bread a soft, melting texture.

5. When you have a fairly smooth ball, pat the top with the oats or wholegrain flour, transfer to a baking tray and then flatten the top slightly. Leave in a warm place for 15 minutes to rise.

6. Use a sharp knife to score the bread into four, cutting almost through to the base, and taking care not to knock the air out.

7. Bake for about 40 minutes until golden brown and cooked through: tap the bottom and it should sound 'hollow'. Set aside to cool on a rack and enjoy warm and fresh on the same day, or freeze.

TRY THIS *You can make individual soda breads in a muffin tin. Weigh out about 75g of the dough onto a square of baking parchment. Drop the dough into 8 holes of a muffin tin and then bake for 30 minutes, or until nicely browned on the top and sides.*

pizza base

Dairy- egg- gluten- and wheat-free, this recipe makes a crust with a great open-bread texture. If you prefer a thin-crust pizza, stretch the dough and either make two or more mini bases.

250g GF White Bread Flour Blend (page 15), or use the quantities below:
45g GF brown rice flour
45g GF white rice flour
80g potato starch
40g GF tapioca flour/starch
40g cornflour

1 level teaspoon xanthan gum (see note on page 27)
½ teaspoon salt
1 teaspoon caster sugar
7g GF fast-action dried yeast
200ml warm water
1 teaspoon apple cider vinegar
1 teaspoon olive oil, plus 2 teaspoons, for brushing

TRY THIS *This flatbread is also good eaten warm on its own as a dipping bread with houmous or oil. Make some dents in the dough just before baking and top it with olive oil, rosemary and sea salt. Bake right through, then cut into slices. Eat it fresh from the oven.*

Makes 1 x 25cm crust · **PREP TIME** *10 minutes, plus 15 minutes proving* · **COOKING TIME** *15 minutes part-baked, plus 10 minutes with topping*

1. Line a baking tray with baking parchment.

2. In a bowl if you're using a hand mixer, or the bowl of a stand mixer, measure the flours, xanthan gum, salt, sugar and yeast, and mix well so they are evenly combined.

3. Add the warm water, vinegar and 1 teaspoon of oil. Beat on low to start, then on high for about 3 minutes to form a soft, smooth and sticky dough. Scrape the mixture down a couple of times to make sure it's fully incorporated.

4. Turn out the dough onto the baking paper and use a spatula to spread it out into an even round about 5mm thick. Build up the edges slightly to contain your topping. Dot the top with the remaining oil and leave it to one side for about 15 minutes while you preheat the oven to 200°C/190°C fan/gas mark 6.

5. Bake for 10–15 minutes until cooked but still a little pale. At this stage you can cool and freeze the part-baked pizza base.

6. Spread the pizza base with sauce and toppings and return it to the hot oven for another 10 minutes until the base is brown and the topping is bubbling. Eat straight away.

Bread Maker Method

In a large bowl, measure the flours, xanthan gum, salt, sugar and yeast, then mix well so they evenly combined to avoid uneven rising. Put the water, vinegar and oil into the bread maker pan, then tip the flour mixture on top. Start the programme on a dough setting. After a couple of minutes, scrape the dough down from the sides of the pan with a plastic spatula, then allow the dough programme to carry on and complete the cycle in the machine. Turn the dough out onto the baking parchment and continue as in the recipe above.

roti

I serve these Indian flatbreads when I want something a bit different with a meal. A very versatile accompaniment, they go perfectly with fish or meat.

150g GF Flour Mix A (page 15),
    or use the quantities below:
100g GF white rice flour
25g potato starch
25g GF tapioca flour/starch

150g GF very fine polenta
¼ level teaspoon guar gum
    (or xanthan gum)
2 tablespoons oil, plus extra
    for greasing
1 small green chilli, very finely
    chopped
1 tablespoon very finely
    chopped ginger
about 150ml hot water
salt and ground black pepper

Makes 4 • **PREP TIME** *15 minutes* • **COOKING TIME** *15 minutes*

1. Place the flours, polenta and guar gum into a bowl. Add a little salt and pepper and mix well. Add the oil, chilli and ginger, and enough water to make a very soft dough. Be careful not to add too much water.

2. Knead well to work in the guar gum and to get a little springiness into the dough. Cover and set aside for a couple of minutes.

3. Heat a griddle or frying pan.

4. Pull off a small lump of dough and flatten it between the palms of your hand. Using a little extra flour, roll it out to 12–15cm across and 5mm thick. Repeat with the remaining dough.

5. Add a drizzle of oil to the pan and cook the roti for a couple of minutes on each side. Stack the cooked breads and cover them loosely with foil to keep them warm.

tortillas

These tortillas are very simple to make. I have added a little xanthan gum to help bring the dough together and make it slightly more forgiving. I use a tortilla press, which you can get online or at cook shops. Otherwise, you can use a rolling pin with pretty good results. I have found that these tortillas need a very hot pan or griddle; I place mine directly onto the hot cooking plate of an Aga.

**200g GF masa harina
   (ground tortilla corn flour)
¼ level teaspoon xanthan gum
a pinch of salt
a pinch of ground black pepper
3–4 tablespoons warm water**

Makes 8–10 tortillas • **PREP TIME** *5 minutes* • **COOKING TIME** *1–2 minutes per tortilla*

1. Put the flour in a bowl and add the gum, salt and pepper. Mix well, then add enough warm water to make a stiff dough.

2. Transfer to a work surface and knead really well for 2–3 minutes, or until the ingredients are thoroughly combined. Wrap in cling film and leave to rest for 10 minutes.

3. Meanwhile, cut some baking parchment or silicone paper to fit the tortilla press. If you don't have a press just prepare two pieces that are about the same size as your griddle, pan or hotplate. Heat the griddle, pan or hot plate to very hot.

4. Place a small amount of dough in between the paper sheets and press or roll until the mix is just coming out from the sides and very thin. A little dough goes a long way, so less is more; you'll be surprised.

5. Carefully peel the paper away from the tortilla and place it straight onto the hot griddle, pan or hot plate. Cook for a few seconds on each side until the tortilla slightly blisters. Set aside on a warm plate and repeat until all the dough is used up.

jalapeño, coriander & Cheddar cornbread

I really like cornbread with chilli or guacamole, lots of fresh coriander, soured cream and refried beans. I find this bread is nicer when it is cooked, cooled and warmed through in a moderate oven or in the microwave.

360g GF masa harina or
fine cornmeal
25g cornflour, arrowroot
or tapioca starch
3 teaspoons GF baking powder
2 teaspoons bicarbonate
of soda
1 teaspoon salt
100g strong Cheddar cheese,
grated
25g chopped fresh chives
25g chopped fresh jalapeño
chillies
25g chopped fresh coriander
340g tin sweetcorn
570ml buttermilk
2 medium eggs

Serves 10 • **PREP TIME** *25 minutes* • **COOKING TIME** *35–45 minutes*

1. Preheat the oven to 180°C/160°C fan/gas mark 4. Lightly grease a 33cm round x 5cm deep non-stick pizza pan, or a similar sized tin.

2. In a bowl, mix together the masa harina, cornflour, baking powder, bicarbonate of soda and salt. Add the cheese, chives, chillies and coriander, and mix well.

3. Blend the sweetcorn with the buttermilk. Add the eggs, but don't over mix, then add the wet ingredients to the dry ones. Mix well.

4. Spoon the mixture into the prepared tin and bake for 30–45 minutes. Once well-risen and browned, remove from the oven and cool on a wire rack.

eggless quinoa chickpea pancakes

This savoury pancake is also known as farinata, socca or cecina and is cooked and served in many countries all over Europe, particularly Italy. Primarily, it uses chickpea (gram) flour and, once mixed, is left to ferment either for a few hours or up to a day or so. The fermenting process not only adds air to the batter but also a lovely, distinct flavour. However, if you can't wait, the addition of a little gluten-free baking powder does a pretty good job.

Cook these pancakes slightly longer than you would a normal pancake, use a little more oil and make sure the pancakes are set in the middle before turning them over. If you're worried they're not cooked through, once the mix is set in the pan and the edges are starting to turn golden, transfer the pan to the oven to finish cooking.

100g GF gram flour
100g GF quinoa flour
½ teaspoon salt
½ teaspoon ground black pepper
a pinch of sugar
450ml warm water
1 teaspoon GF baking powder (optional)
50ml extra virgin olive oil, plus 2–3 tablespoons, for greasing

Makes 4–6 pancakes • **PREP TIME** *5 minutes, plus up to 12 hours to ferment* • **COOKING TIME** *20 minutes*

1. If you're going to finish cooking the pancakes in the oven, preheat it to 230°C/gas mark 8.

2. In a bowl, whisk together the flours, salt, pepper and sugar. Add the warm water and whisk well. Cover and leave in a warm place for a few hours to ferment. Alternatively, add the baking powder to the mixture and continue to the next step.

3. Whisk in the olive oil until fully incorporated.

4. Add 2–3 tablespoons olive oil to a non-stick frying pan over a high heat. Once the oil is just smoking, pour in a ladleful of batter, swirling it around the pan to cover the base; it should be 3–4mm thick. The edges will bubble and brown very quickly.

5. Once the centre is dry to the touch (this is very important or the pancake can break) use a spatula or palette knife to carefully flip it over to cook the other side (or pop the pan in the oven to cook the top). Continue to cook the pancakes, piling them up on the plate to keep them warm.

6. Eat warm or cover with cling film and refrigerate until needed.

rich pasta dough

This pasta needs to be cooked while fresh because if it dries out it gets brittle and shatters. It will roll well with a simple rolling pin, but knead well first. You could make it into noodles using a pasta machine or by hand.

160g GF fine white rice flour,
    plus extra for dusting
60g GF custard powder
20g cornflour
a pinch of salt
1 level teaspoon xanthan gum
4 tablespoons olive oil
2 medium eggs
2 medium egg yolks

Makes about 400g • **PREP TIME** *10 minutes* • **RESTING TIME** *10 minutes*

1. Place the rice flour, custard powder, cornflour, salt and xanthan gum into a food-processor. Pulse for a few seconds to incorporate well. Add the oil, eggs and yolks along with 3 tablespoons of cold water, and pulse until you have nice firm dough.

2. Remove from the processor and knead on a lightly dusted surface to bring the dough together. Cover with cling film and chill for 10 minutes.

3. Knead again for about 30 seconds, then roll out on a dusted work surface until the dough is nice and thin. Cut and shape it as desired.

4. Cook straight away in plenty of boiling salted water for 3–4 minutes. Strain this pasta well once cooked and rinse with a little boiling water. This removes any excess starch or rolling-out flour. If you don't, it can leave a gummy mouthfeel when eaten. It can be dried for storage, but it is prone to shattering.

TIP *For me, custard powder does the job perfectly, but if you don't want to use custard powder to colour the pasta, replace it with cornflour and add natural ground annatto or beta carotene.*

TIP *When rolling gluten-free pasta you have to roll it slightly thinner than you would for normal pasta as it tends to swell slightly when cooked. Some people recommend dusting the work surface with starch to aid rolling, but I tend not to use any as it can give the cooked pasta a gluey texture.*

classic shortcrust pastry

As with all pastry making, patience is a virtue when you set off down the gluten-free road. Work quickly and lightly with the pastry dough. For the lightest pastry, you are aiming for softer than normal dough that holds together well, but is not wet.

200g GF White and Brown Rice Flour Blend (page 15)
a pinch of salt
½ level teaspoon xanthan gum
100g cold butter or dairy-free baking margarine, cut into rough pieces
1 small egg, beaten
1 teaspoon lemon juice

Makes about 350g or enough for 1 x 22cm tart • **PREP TIME** *15 minutes*

1. Put the flour, salt, xanthan gum and butter or margarine into a food-processor and pulse until you have a fine crumb texture. (You can rub in by hand but it will warm the mixture up and it may melt quickly, so you may need to chill it before rolling.)

2. Add the beaten egg, 1–2 tablespoons of cold water and the lemon juice, then pulse until the mixture just starts to hold together in small clumps. If it seems dry, add an extra teaspoon of water; you want a soft dough that holds together well but is not wet.

3. Roll out a sheet of cling film and tip the pastry dough onto it. Lay another sheet of cling film over the top and roll the pastry into a disc, then chill, wrapped in the cling film, for no longer than 15 minutes, until firmer but not hard. Now you're ready to roll.

almond pastry
Swap 25g of the flour for 25g of ground almonds. You may need to adjust the amount of water to use.

TIP *A cool room temperature is ideal for rolling this pastry. If your dough is too sticky, pop it back in the fridge to chill for 10 minutes; if it's too hard to roll and breaks, let it warm up a little. The lemon juice makes the dough a touch more elastic for rolling.*

gluten-free shortcrust pastry

If you don't have xanthan gum you can substitute 2 teaspoons of gluten-free psyllium husk, but you will need to add a little more water as it has a higher absorption rate.

225g GF Flour Mix A (page 15)
2 pinches of salt
1 level teaspoon xanthan gum
110g dairy-free baking
  margarine, cut into rough
  pieces
1 medium egg, beaten

Makes about 375g or enough for 1 x 24cm x 4cm deep tart
• PREP TIME *10 minutes*

1. Put the flour, salt and xanthan gum into a bowl and mix well. Add the margarine and rub in until you have fine breadcrumbs (or use a food-processor).

2. Add the beaten egg and a little cold water, and mix really well. Keep an eye on the texture – you may need to add a little more water so that it is nice and soft. Bear in mind that the gum will tighten up the mixture considerably.

3. Roll out and use.

TIP *If you want to keep pastry for longer, or freeze it, make sure you let the pastry come to room temperature before using or it will be too hard to roll.*

sweet shortcrust pastry

If you like your pastry just a touch sweeter than savoury, you can sweeten the Classic Shortcrust Pastry recipe on page 40 by adding a tablespoon of icing sugar in with the flour. This version is sweeter, for tarts that you plan to fill with chocolate, custard or fresh fruit.

175g GF White and Brown Rice
    Flour Blend (page 15)
¼ level teaspoon xanthan gum
40g icing sugar
75g cold butter or dairy-free
    baking margarine, cut into
    rough pieces
1 small egg, beaten

Makes about 325g dough or enough for 1 x 20cm tart or 12 small pies
• **PREP TIME** *15 minutes*

1. Put the flour, xanthan gum, sugar and butter or margarine into a food-processor and pulse until you have a fine powder. (You can rub this in by hand but it will warm the mixture up and it may melt quickly, so you need to chill it before rolling.)

2. Add most of the beaten egg and pulse just until the mixture starts to hold together in small clumps. If it seems dry, add an extra teaspoon of water. For the lightest pastry, you are aiming for soft dough that holds together well, but is not wet.

3. It's easier to roll the pastry between two sheets of cling film: tip the pastry dough onto a sheet of cling film and then roll it to a disc. Wrap the disc in cling film and chill for about 15 minutes, until firm but not rock hard. Now you're ready to roll.

See the Classic Shortcrust Pastry recipe on page 40 for useful tips.

sweet chocolate shortcrust pastry

This pastry is not super-sweet, so it's great as a base to offset a sweet chocolate mousse filling. Try it also with a banoffee filling spread with caramel and banana, or as a contrast for a meringue pie or cheesecake. Find a good, dark cocoa powder for a full, intense chocolate flavour.

125g GF White and Brown Rice Flour Blend (page 15)
25g cocoa powder
¼ level teaspoon xanthan gum
25g icing sugar
75g cold butter or dairy-free baking margarine, cut into rough pieces
1 small egg, beaten

Makes about 325g or enough for 1 x 20cm tart or 12 tartlets
• **PREP TIME** *15 minutes, plus 30 minutes chilling* • **COOKING TIME** *12–15 minutes*

1. Sift the flour, cocoa powder, xanthan gum and icing sugar and tip it into a food-processor with the butter or margarine. Pulse until you have a fine crumb texture. (You can rub in by hand but it will warm the mixture up and it may melt quickly, so you may need to chill it before rolling.)

2. Add the egg and pulse until the mixture just starts to hold together; in small clumps. For the lightest pastry, you are aiming for soft dough that holds together well but is not wet.

3. It's easier to roll the pastry between two sheets of cling film: tip out the pastry dough, bring it together with your hands and then flatten it into a disc. Wrap in cling film and chill for about 20 minutes until firm but not rock hard. It is now ready to roll.

TIP *For tartlets, roll the dough really thin. You can use a muffin tray to shape them: cut rounds larger than the holes and lower the pastry in gently. Prick the base and bake for about 12 minutes at 190°C/180°C fan/gas mark 5.*

See the Classic Shortcrust Pastry recipe on page 40 for more useful tips.

rough puff pastry

This is a cross between flaky and puff pastry. Try it with the Sausage Rolls (opposite), or for a delicious pie crust. It's not difficult to make you just need time and patience. The recipe makes a generous amount so you can use what you need and freeze the rest. Make sure the butter is very cold and hard. You want to trap little pieces in the dough, which melt during cooking. The water from the butter evaporates as it cooks and turns to steam, rising and pushing up the layers to create the flake. A little cold lard (15g) substituted for butter adds flavour.

250g GF White and Brown Rice Flour Blend (page 15)
½ level teaspoon xanthan gum
¼ teaspoon GF baking powder
a pinch of salt
1 tablespoon olive oil
150g very cold butter, cut into small cubes
1 teaspoon lemon juice

Makes about 550g · **PREP TIME** *1½ hours, with chilling time*

1. Put the flour, xanthan gum, baking powder and salt into a bowl. Mix the oil through until it disappears. Tip in the butter and stir in with the blade of a knife (your hands will be too warm).

2. Pour 125–150ml of cold water and the lemon juice over the dry mixture, and mix without kneading to form a soft, lumpy dough. Cover in cling film and chill for 15 minutes.

3. Tip the dough onto a sheet of baking parchment or cling film and lay a second sheet on top. Roll it out to a rectangle about 20 x 30cm. Keep to a light and even movement, rolling back and forth, and giving the pastry a quarter turn as it gets thinner. Knock the edges into shape.

4. Now you need to create layers of air in the dough by folding and rerolling it. Take one end of the dough and fold it in on itself to the middle. Fold the opposite end in to meet the other fold, then fold again, like a book.

5. Roll and fold again, then wrap and chill for 20 minutes.

6. Repeat this rolling, folding and chilling twice more before rolling the dough out to bake with. You can freeze the pastry at this point. Wrap it well in cling film and freeze pre-rolled. Defrost to room temperature before using.

TIP *Bake rough puff in a really hot oven and leave lots of space around the edges. An egg, beaten with 1 teaspoon of cold water and a pinch of salt, brushed over the top (but clear of the edges) before baking will give it a nice glaze.*

rough puff sausage rolls

If you happen to have a sheet of rough puff in the freezer, these little bite-sized sausage rolls make excellent use of it as the crisp, flaky outer layers work wonderfully with the juicy filling. I've suggested a few interesting additions for more flavour. You can also make these with shortcrust or a more simple flaky pastry, to save time.

550g Rough Puff Pastry (opposite)
450g GF sausages
1 small egg
a pinch of salt

Makes about 14 mini rolls • **PREP TIME** *15 minutes* • **COOKING TIME** *40 minutes*

1. Preheat the oven to 200°C/190°C fan/gas mark 6. Line a baking tray with tin foil or parchment paper.

2. Lay a sheet of cling film on a work surface and put the pastry on top. Roll out the dough to a rough 30cm square, about 5mm thick. Trim the edges and cut into two strips about 15cm wide. Keep the pastry cold and avoid handling it too much. If it gets too soft, pop it back in the fridge for a bit to firm up.

3. Slice through the sausage skins with a sharp knife and squeeze the meat out of the casings. Place the meat down the centre of each pastry strip.

4. Brush the edges of the pastry with cold water and roll them up around the fillings to enclose. Cut 4cm sausage rolls and lay them on the prepared baking tray seam-side down, leaving lots of space around each roll.

5. Make a couple of diagonal slits on the top of each roll for decoration, then beat together the egg with 1 teaspoon of cold water and a pinch of salt to make an egg wash and brush the tops of the sausage rolls to glaze them. Don't brush right to the edges, though, to allow the pastry to flake up.

6. Bake for 30–40 minutes until brown and glistening on top.

TRY THIS *You can add a variety of flavours to make the sausagemeat more interesting. Mix in some chopped fresh thyme and a small very finely chopped onion for added flavour. The sausage rolls can be spicy with the addition of a pinch of chilli flakes to the meat, or smoky, seasoned with paprika. Or mix in a tablespoon of caramelised onions or red onion marmalade, chopped apple or gluten-free chutney.*

TIP *Rough or puff pastry is better if you don't re-roll the trimmings. Use them up by making simple pastry twists or cheese straws, sprinkled with paprika and herbs or chopped sun-dried tomatoes.*

rich tart pastry

I use this delicious pastry for chocolate tarts or savoury flans. It's richer than the previous pastry recipes and slightly crumbly. The addition of sour cream gives the pastry a different kind of texture and 'snap'. You may sometimes get a very slight cracking on the top lip as it's where the pastry is at its thinnest, but this is simply remedied by gently pressing the dough together.

180g GF Sorghum Flour Blend (page 15), plus extra for dusting
½ level teaspoon xanthan gum
a pinch of salt
90g dairy-free baking margarine, cut into rough pieces
40g soured cream
1 tablespoon white wine vinegar
1 medium egg yolk

Makes 1 x 23cm x 4cm-deep tart · **PREP TIME** *15 minutes*

1. Put the flour, xanthan gum and salt into a food-processor with the margarine and pulse until you have a fine crumb texture.

2. In a bowl mix together the soured cream, vinegar and egg yolk with 2 tablespoons cold water. Pour the wet mixture into the processor and pulse everything together well. The mix will come together nicely. Remove and knead gently, then chill for 10 minutes.

3. Dust the work surface with a little gluten-free flour and roll out the pastry. It rolls well without the need for baking parchment or cling film.

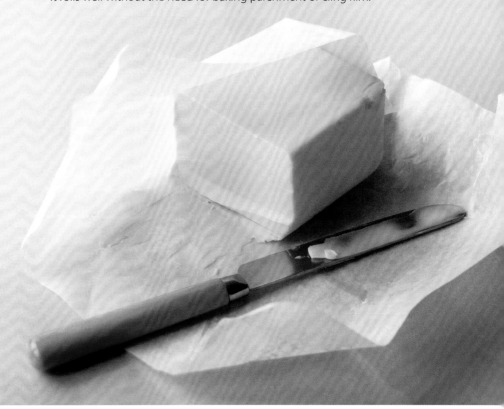

choux pastry

This makes very nice profiteroles or éclairs. A few points to remember though: I find beating the boiled paste straight away vigorously in a machine helps. Adding the first two eggs slowly ensures a soft texture. Then add the remaining eggs until you have a firm texture that will fall from a spatula in 10 seconds or so. This recipe makes about 600g of choux pastry; it works just as well using half the quantities.

a pinch of salt
100g hard baking margarine
    (or butter), melted
130g GF Flour Mix A (page 15)
3 medium eggs, at room
    temperature, beaten

Makes about 20–30 small buns or éclairs • **PREP TIME** *20 minutes* • **COOKING TIME** *30 minutes*

1. Pre heat the oven to 220°C/200°C fan/gas mark 7.

2. Bring 250ml of water and the salt to the boil in a medium saucepan, then add the melted margarine. Immediately add the flour to the mixture, remove the pan from the heat and beat well until incorporated.

3. Pop the mixture into the bowl of a stand mixer straight away, and beat with a paddle on a medium speed for 2–3 minutes until soft and well mixed.

4. While still just warm, gradually add two beaten eggs, a little at a time, and beat on a high speed until smooth. This may take a couple of minutes.

5. Next, gradually add the remaining egg and beat until the mixture just falls off a spoon when lifted: you may not need all the egg and too much can affect the rise.

6. Line a couple of baking trays with baking parchment. Fill a large piping bag, fitted with a plain nozzle, with the choux paste. Pipe while still warm into the shape you require, spaced evenly apart. If they come out unevenly shaped, you can reshape them using a pastry brush dipped in beaten egg.

7. Cook for 25–30 minutes until well risen and nicely coloured. Give them an extra 5 minutes to unsure the insides are totally dry.

8. Remove from the oven and cool. You are now ready to fill your buns.

TIP *Make sure you melt the margarine in a separate pan or in the microwave. If you wait to melt it in the boiling water you can lose as much as 10 per cent of the water, changing the complex structure of the end result and leaving you with heavy, greasy buns.*

snacks, salads & sides

carrot, cashew & pomegranate salad

FOR THE SALAD

2 large carrots, peeled and
  sliced into very fine strips

1 small red onion, very finely
  sliced

4 tablespoons salted cashew
  nuts, chopped, plus 50g
  to finish

4 tablespoons roughly
  chopped fresh mint

unsmoked or smoked paprika,
  for sprinkling

FOR THE DRESSING

2 tablespoons pomegranate
  molasses

4 tablespoons extra virgin
  olive oil

juice of 1 large lime

1 tablespoon sherry vinegar

salt and ground black pepper

I once had a version of this simple salad in a market in Tel Aviv; it was so easy to prepare. It's perfect for lunch with a little grilled chicken or fish.

Serves 4 • **PREP TIME** *20 minutes*

1. First make the dressing by placing all the ingredients in a large bowl and whisking well.

2. Next, add all the vegetables, mint and chopped nuts, and mix thoroughly. You may need to add more seasoning. Leave at room temperature for 15–20 minutes, stirring occasionally.

3. Serve dusted with a little paprika and the whole cashew nuts.

avocado, shrimp & peanut salad with Thai basil and lime

4 ripe, waxy avocados, stones
  removed

juice of 2 large limes, plus
  1 lime, quartered, to serve

1 small bunch of Thai basil,
  roughly chopped

salt and ground black pepper

a pinch of sugar

250g brown shrimps or small
  prawns, shelled

100g GF dry-roasted peanuts,
  roughly chopped

GF rice crackers, to serve

This is such a simple but delicious recipe. I normally use a smooth-skinned avocado for this salad as I find the flesh is creamier and smoother. It's a unique match of some of my favourite flavours and textures.

Serves 4 • **PREP TIME** *15 minutes*

1. Score the flesh of the avocado halves in long slices and scoop out the flesh with a spoon. Place in a bowl and coat with the lime juice. Add the basil and season well with salt, pepper and the sugar. Finally add the shrimps or prawns.

2. Spoon the salad into small bowls and sprinkle over the chopped peanuts. Serve with rice crackers and more lime wedges.

chicory & pear salad with cambozola yogurt dressing

The combination of a few simple ingredients can sometimes make a lovely dish. This is a classic example. Take care as mustard isn't always gluten-free and it could have been contaminated during production. Make sure you check the label before using.

Serves 2 · **PREP TIME** *10 minutes*

FOR THE SALAD

1 head of Belgium chicory

1 head of radicchio or red Belgian chicory

2 ripe Williams pears, peeled, cored and finely sliced

1 small orange, peeled, segmented and roughly chopped

150g cambozola cheese, cut into 2cm pieces, or a semi-soft light blue-veined cheese

50g lightly toasted pecans, roughly chopped

FOR THE DRESSING

100g Greek yogurt

2 tablespoons sherry vinegar

1 teaspoon GF Dijon mustard

2 tablespoons extra virgin olive oil

salt and ground black pepper

1. In a bowl, whisk together all the ingredients for the salad dressing and season well with salt and pepper.

2. Finely slice the chicory and radicchio on the diagonal and toss into a bowl. Add the pears, orange and cheese, and lightly mix. Drizzle over the dressing and mix well.

3. Serve topped with the toasted pecans. It's as easy as that.

simple quinoa, cashew & tomato salad

For this deceptively simple salad or starter to work, the tomatoes need to be at room temperature and very ripe, plus the quinoa, which gives the salad substance, should be warm. I also sometimes add a little grilled fish or meat to make a main course.

12 medium tomatoes, at room
temperature, quartered
200g salted cashews, whole
500g cooked quinoa, warm
4–5 tablespoons extra virgin
olive oil
2–3 tablespoons balsamic
vinegar
salt and ground black pepper
about 100g finely grated fresh
Parmesan cheese

Serves 4 • **PREP TIME** *10 minutes* • **COOKING TIME** *15 minutes*

1. Place the tomatoes in a bowl and mix with the cashews. Add the warm quinoa and mix lightly. Add the oil and vinegar and season well with salt and pepper. Again, lightly mix.

2. Spoon into bowls, scatter with the grated cheese and serve straight away. That's it!

TIP *I like to use a mix of white and red quinoa for this salad. Some ready-cooked sachets work quite well; just pop them in the microwave for 2 minutes to heat up. Be sure to check they are gluten-free.*

pink grapefruit, lime, green bean & chilli cabbage salad with chicken & prawns

FOR THE SALAD

1 red onion, very finely sliced

1 pink grapefruit, segmented

¼ large white, firm cabbage, very thinly sliced

8 flat or runner stringless beans, cut into thin slices

1 small red chilli, very finely chopped

30g piece of ginger, peeled and cut into very thin strips

2 medium skinless chicken breasts, cut into 2 cm pieces

8 freshwater prawns, shelled and halved lengthways

FOR THE DRESSING

6 tablespoons sunflower oil

juice of 2 large limes

juice of 1 pink grapefruit

1 tablespoon palm or soft brown sugar

salt and ground black pepper

This very tasty summer salad is best made one hour before eating and then left for the flavours to combine. It's ideal served as a starter and is a snappy way for the kids to eat raw vegetables. The vegetables need to be sliced really thinly so use a mandolin, if you have one.

Serves 4 · **PREP TIME** *10 minutes*

1. In a bowl, mix together all the ingredients for the salad, except for the chicken and prawns.

2. In a separate small bowl, whisk together all the ingredients for the dressing and season well with salt and pepper. Pour over the salad, then leave at room temperature for 30 minutes.

3. Meanwhile, sauté the chicken breasts for 3 minutes in a hot pan, add the prawns and cook for a further 2 minutes, or until lightly cooked. Do not overcook.

4. Serve the salad in deep bowls, topped with the chicken and prawns.

rice noodle salad with sautéed sweet potato, peppers & squash

FOR THE SALAD

4 tablespoons vegetable oil

1 small sweet potato, peeled and finely chopped

½ small butternut squash, peeled, deseeded and finely chopped

1 red pepper, deseeded and finely chopped

1 yellow pepper, deseeded and finely chopped

200g GF fine rice noodles

150g beansprouts

4 tablespoons chopped fresh coriander

FOR THE DRESSING

1 tablespoon GF brown miso paste

2 tablespoons mirin

1 teaspoon chopped fresh red chilli

1 tablespoon olive oil

2 tablespoons rice wine vinegar

1 garlic clove, finely crushed

salt and ground black pepper

This is a tasty salad that's really good for you. It's light and packed full of proteins and vegetables. I sometimes have it for lunch topped with a few cooked prawns or with a little leftover roast chicken sliced up and mixed through. It will keep for a few days, covered in the fridge. Rice noodles are easy to digest, easy to cook and give bulk to your meals if you are following a gluten-free diet.

Serves 4 • **PREP TIME** *25 minutes* • **COOKING TIME** *30 minutes*

1. Heat the oil for the salad in a large frying pan or wok over a medium heat. Fry all the vegetables, except for the beansprouts, until lightly cooked. Season well with salt and pepper, then keep warm.

2. Bring a saucepan of water to the boil and add a little salt. Plunge in the noodles and cook according to packet instructions until soft, then drain well. Mix with the warm vegetables.

3. Make the dressing by mixing all the ingredients together well.

4. When ready to serve, pour the dressing over the vegetables and noodles, and mix well. Add the beansprouts and chopped coriander and mix well again. Serve in deep bowls.

crispy fried smoked mackerel salad

FOR THE SALAD

1 small carrot, peeled and
finely sliced

4 green beans such as runner
beans, finely sliced

4 shallots, finely sliced

3 smoked mackerel fillets,
skinned, boned and flaked

2–3 tablespoons cornflour

vegetable oil, for frying

a handful of GF honey-roasted
cashews

2 tablespoons chopped fresh
coriander

4 tablespoons chopped fresh
Thai basil

FOR THE DRESSING

½ small red chilli

1 tablespoon nam pla fish
sauce

1 garlic clove, very finely
crushed

2 tablespoons palm sugar,
(crushed if bought in a block)

finely grated zest and juice
of 2 large limes

The smoked, sweet mackerel works really well in this recipe, but a little fish goes a long way, so don't overload the salad with fish. The rest is a simple combination of lovely flavours and textures.

Serves 2–4 • **PREP TIME** *15 minutes* • **COOKING TIME** *20 minutes*

1. Place the carrot, green beans and shallots in a bowl, and mix well.

2. In a separate bowl, mix together all the dressing ingredients.

3. Dust the flaked fish in the cornflour.

4. Heat the oil in a shallow frying pan.

5. Add small amounts of the mackerel and cook for 2–3 minutes until very crispy.

6. When ready to serve, add the dressing to the carrot salad, then add the cashews, coriander and basil, and mix well. Finally, add the cooked crispy fish. Serve straight away.

TIP *Dusting the fish in cornflour stops the oil spitting and spluttering; it also helps to give a slightly crispier edge. Arrowroot works equally well, as does tapioca flour.*

warm summer salmon, vegetable & peanut salad

I find a combination of hot and cold ingredients in a salad makes it a lot more appealing. Here the salmon and vegetables are cooked in the same pan, saving time, utensils and energy.

6 tablespoons olive oil
1 red onion, roughly chopped
2 red peppers, deseeded and
   chopped into 2cm pieces
200g mangetout or sugar
   snaps
200g fine green beans
2 tablespoons cider vinegar
4 x 150g salmon fillets, skin on
1 garlic clove, finely chopped
4 heaped tablespoons GF
   mayonnaise
4 ripe tomatoes, chopped
1 small head of lettuce such
   as iceberg or cos
2 tablespoons chopped
   GF salted peanuts
juice of 2 fresh limes
salt and ground black pepper

Serves 4 · **PREP TIME** *10 minutes* · **COOKING TIME** *20 minutes*

1. Heat half the olive oil in a pan over a medium heat. Add the onion and red peppers, and cook for 5 minutes until softened and coloured slightly.

2. Bring a pan of salted water to the boil and cook the mangetout and green beans until tender. Remove with a slotted spoon and add the vinegar to the water.

3. Drop in the salmon fillets, bring back to a simmer, then immediately turn off the heat. Leave the salmon for 10 minutes, by which time it will be cooked perfectly.

4. Meanwhile, in a small bowl, stir the garlic into the mayonnaise.

5. In a separate bowl, mix together the onion and pepper, the mangetout and beans, the tomatoes, salad leaves, peanuts, lime juice, salt and pepper.

6. Divide the salad between four bowls or plates, top with a piece of salmon and serve with the garlic mayonnaise on the side.

salade niçoise

This classic salad from the south of France is full of flavour. The hard work is in the prep, but once that's done it's easy to put together.

Serves 4–6 · **PREP TIME** *15 minutes* · **COOKING TIME** *10 minutes*

FOR THE SALAD

1 head of cos lettuce, washed, drained and chopped

1 large potato, boiled in skin, cooled, peeled and cubed

4 ripe plum tomatoes, cut into chunks

4 hard-boiled eggs, peeled and quartered

200g tin tuna in oil, drained

16 pitted black olives

FOR THE DRESSING

1 teaspoon GF Dijon mustard

3 tablespoons sherry vinegar

a pinch of ground black pepper

4 tablespoons extra virgin olive oil

2 tablespoons sunflower oil

10 anchovy fillets, roughly chopped

4 tablespoons roughly chopped flat-leaf parsley

1. To make the dressing, mix together the mustard, vinegar and black pepper in a small bowl. Gradually add the oils, mixing well. Add the anchovies and parsley.

2. Put all the salad ingredients into a large bowl and mix gently but thoroughly, carefully breaking up the tuna into bite-sized chunks.

3. Pour over the dressing and toss everything together. Serve straight away.

easy turkey caesar

I had to include a version of this universally acclaimed salad somewhere in this book. I find that gluten-free bread makes lovely croûtons and I rather like to eat this salad without any turkey as a light main course. I use fresh egg yolks, but pasteurised yolks are a perfectly acceptable substitute, although you may need to use a little extra to get the same result.

4 tablespoons olive oil

3 slices of stale GF white
   bread, cubed

4 x 115g turkey breasts, sliced

1 small head of cos lettuce, or
   2 Little Gems, roughly sliced

75g Parmesan cheese

FOR THE DRESSING

2 medium egg yolks

1 garlic clove, crushed

1 tablespoon white wine
   vinegar or cider vinegar

a pinch of ground black pepper

3 teaspoons GF Dijon mustard

4 salted anchovy fillets

200ml olive oil

Serves 4 · **PREP TIME** *15 minutes* · **COOKING TIME** *10 minutes*

1. First make the dressing. Blitz the egg yolks, garlic, vinegar, pepper, mustard and anchovies in a liquidiser until smooth. Add the oil in a thin stream, continuing to pulse. The dressing should coat the leaves nicely, but not be too thick, so add a little water until you have the right consistency. Check the seasoning.

2. Heat half the oil in a frying pan and sauté the bread cubes until crisp and golden. Set aside.

3. Add the rest of the oil to the pan and sauté the turkey slices for 2–3 minutes on each side until just cooked, then keep warm.

4. Dress the leaves and stir through the croûtons.

5. Serve in deep bowls topped with the warm turkey slices and the Parmesan shaved over the top.

sautéed parsley new potatoes

This is a twist on the classic French Lyonnaise potatoes, which are sautéed with finely sliced onions. Here I've added parsley.

500g new or salad potatoes, halved
3 tablespoons vegetable oil
1 medium onion, finely sliced
4 tablespoons chopped parsley
salt and ground black pepper

Serves 4 · **PREP TIME** *15 minutes* · **COOKING TIME** *20 minutes*

1. Put the potatoes in a pan of cold salted water and bring to the boil. Simmer until cooked, then drain well.

2. Heat 2 tablespoons of the oil in a frying pan, add the onion and cook for 10 minutes until softened. Remove from the pan.

3. Add the remaining oil and the drained potatoes to the pan and fry gently for 15 minutes, or until nicely browned all over.

4. Tip the onion back into the pan with the parsley and season with salt and pepper.

saffron, new potato & tarragon salad

This colourful salad is a nice accompaniment to grilled fish, roasted chicken, cold ham, or topped with a poached or soft-boiled egg.

500g baby new potatoes, halved
a small pinch of saffron threads
4 tablespoons boiling water
570ml GF mayonnaise
6 tablespoons finely chopped fresh tarragon
4–6 tablespoons lemon juice
salt and ground black pepper

Serves 4 • **PREP TIME** *20 minutes* • **COOKING TIME** *20 minutes*

1. Put the potatoes in a pan of cold salted water and bring to the boil. Lower the heat and gently simmer for 10–12 minutes until cooked. Drain well, then cover with cling film and set aside to cool.

2. Meanwhile, steep the saffron threads in the boiling water until the wonderful colour has been extracted from the saffron.

3. Put the mayonnaise in a large bowl and whisk in the saffron and cooled water. Add the tarragon and lemon juice, and season well with salt and pepper.

4. Once the potatoes are at room temperature, add them to the mayonnaise mixture and mix thoroughly.

TIP *Covering the potatoes with cling film really helps to retain their flavour as they cool.*

chips

500g potatoes such as King Edward, Maris Piper, Red Rooster, Wilja or Marfona
groundnut, safflower or sunflower oil, for deep-frying (see note about contamination on page 8)
salt and vinegar, to serve (optional)

Makes 500g • **PREP TIME** *10 minutes* • **COOKING TIME** *15–20 minutes*

1. Peel and wash the potatoes well, then cut into fingers 1.5cm thick. Wash again and dry well on kitchen paper.

2. In a deep-sided pan or deep-fat fryer, heat the oil to 190°C. Let it sit for 10 minutes, then reduce to 175°C. Never fill a fryer more than two-thirds full. If you're using a pan on the hob, never leave it unattended.

3. Using a slotted spoon, plunge a few chips into the oil and cook for 3–4 minutes so that they are softened but not coloured. Shake off the excess oil and cool on a tray lined with kitchen paper in an even layer. Repeat with the rest of the chips. You can chill them at this point.

4. When ready to serve, heat the oil to 185–190°C and cook the chips in small batches until crisp and golden. Drain well on kitchen paper and season with salt and vinegar, if liked.

crispy deep-fried beans

This recipe also works well with thin-cut vegetables such as courgettes, sweet potatoes, parsnips, carrots and so on. Blanching the vegetables first makes a big difference to the end result. I use gluten-free lager for a lot of my batters and it works extremely well, but fizzy water is a good alternative. Remember to fry in several batches to keep the heat in the oil.

450g fine green beans, topped and tailed
1½ tablespoons olive oil
2 small shallots, chopped
200g GF yellow bean sauce
vegetable oil, for deep-frying (see note about contamination on page 8)
225g GF self-raising flour
salt and ground black pepper
300ml GF lager or sparkling water
100g rocket leaves, to serve
12 spring onions, trimmed and cut into strips, to serve

Serves 4–6 • **PREP TIME** *10 minutes* • **COOKING TIME** *8–10 minutes*

1. Bring a pan of cold salted water to a rapid boil and blanch the beans for 1 minute. Drain, then refresh under cold running water.

2. Heat 1 tablespoon of the olive oil in a small frying pan. Cook the shallots gently until softened.

3. Tip the yellow bean sauce into a bowl, stir in the cooked shallots and the remaining ½ tablespoon of olive oil. If necessary, add a little cold water to thin the sauce down slightly.

4. Heat the vegetable oil to 185°C in a deep-fat fryer or deep-sided pan filled one-third full.

5. Sift the flour into a large bowl and season it with salt and pepper. Beat in the lager or water to make a smooth batter, adding a little more water if the batter is too thick.

6. Dip the beans into the batter to coat, then deep-fry for 3–4 minutes, or until cooked and crisp.

7. Arrange the rocket leaves on plates and drizzle over the yellow bean dressing. Pile the beans in the centre and top with the spring onions.

simple braised rice

Brown rice is packed with nutrients and fibre. You can also make this with a mixture of rice and quinoa.

200g brown rice, or a mix of 150g brown rice and 50g quinoa, soaked overnight in cold water

2 tablespoons olive oil, plus 1 tablespoon or a knob of butter

1 small onion, finely chopped

400ml boiling water (or double the volume of water to rice)

1 GF stock cube, chicken, vegetable or beef

salt and ground black pepper

Serves 4 · **PREP TIME** *5 minutes* · **COOKING TIME** *25 minutes*

1. Preheat the oven to 180°C /160°C fan/gas mark 4. Drain the rice (or rice and quinoa); If you haven't soaked the rice, it may take a little longer to cook.

2. Heat 2 tablespoons of the oil in an ovenproof pan and cook the onion for 2 minutes. Add the rice and coat well in the oil and onion. Pour in the boiling water and sprinkle in the stock cube. Stir and bring back to the boil.

3. Put the lid on the pan and place it in the oven for 25–30 minutes until the rice is cooked.

4. Remove the pan, stir well and add the remaining oil or butter. Season with salt and lots of pepper, and leave to sit covered for 5 minutes before serving.

Yorkshire puddings

This recipe makes really light, fluffy puds. They won't be as high as normal Yorkies, but they'll be pretty close. It's essential that the oven, tray and oil are very hot to get the initial lift, and make sure you mix again well just before you pour the batter into the hot oil as the mixture will immediately start to separate due to lack of gluten.

80g GF Flour Mix A (page 15)

55g cornflour

a pinch of salt

3 medium eggs

150ml milk or water

oil, for greasing

Makes 12 · **PREP TIME** *10 minutes* · **COOKING TIME** *35–45 minutes*

1. Preheat the oven to 220°C/gas mark 7. Lightly oil a 12-hole muffin tray and heat in the oven for 10–12 minutes until just smoking.

2. Meanwhile, put the flour mix, cornflour and salt into a bowl and make a small well in the centre. Add the eggs and half the milk, and whisk well until fully incorporated. Add the rest of the milk and mix well again. Immediately pour the batter into the smoking hot muffin tray so that the holes are no more than half full.

3. Cook for 15–20 minutes then reduce the heat to 200°C/gas mark 6. Cook for a further 15 minutes until nicely brown and set.

microwave spring green hearts with hazelnut butter sauce

This sauce works well with all green vegetables and is also lovely served with poached fish or chicken.

2 medium spring greens, outer leaves removed
salt and ground black pepper

FOR THE SAUCE
2 tablespoons white wine vinegar
100ml dry white wine
1 small onion, very finely chopped
a pinch of salt and ground black pepper
55–75g cold butter, cut into small cubes
75g hazelnuts, roasted and chopped

Serves 4 · **PREP TIME** *20 minutes* · **COOKING TIME** *10 minutes*

1. Start by making the sauce. Bring the vinegar, white wine, onion, salt and pepper to the boil in a pan over a high heat. Cook down until you are left with 2–3 tablespoons of liquid.

2. Remove the pan from the heat and gradually add the butter, whisking continuously. The sauce will thicken naturally. Check the seasoning and adjust if needed, then add the hazelnuts. Cover and keep warm.

3. Cut the spring greens in half lengthways and place them cut-side down on two microwavable plates. Season well with salt and pepper, add a dash of cold water and cover with cling film. Make a couple of incisions in the top.

4. Cook on full power, one plate at a time, for 3–4 minutes. Drain well on kitchen paper.

5. Serve sliced or whole on warm plates and spoon over the sauce at the last minute.

TIP *The secret to this sauce is to reduce the vinegar and wine until you have a syrupy consistency, then whisk in the very cold butter in small amounts so that the sauce thickens nicely.*

TIP *You don't have to use nuts for this recipe – chives, tomatoes, parsley and mushrooms all work really well.*

roast tandoori whole cauliflower

200g GF Greek yogurt
1 tablespoon GF garam masala
1 teaspoon dried chilli flakes
½ teaspoon ground cumin
½ teaspoon ground turmeric
½ teaspoon dried garlic
   powder or granules
salt and ground black pepper
1 medium cauliflower, leaves
   and stem removed but left
   whole
4 tablespoons GF spicy mango
   chutney, to serve
2 tablespoons chopped fresh
   coriander, to garnish
2 tablespoons chopped fresh
   mint, to garnish

I'm not sure where I first saw this method for cooking cauliflower, but I think it's really clever. The baking process really holds in all the flavour and it's nice to serve up the whole cauliflower and let guests help themselves.

Serves 4 · **PREP TIME** *10 minutes* · **COOKING TIME** *about 1 hour*

1. Preheat the oven to 200°C/gas mark 6. Line a baking tray or ovenproof frying pan with a double layer of foil.

2. Mix the yogurt with all the spices, the garlic and a little salt and pepper.

3. Place the cauliflower in the centre of the tray or pan and spoon over the thick yogurt mixture, coating really well.

4. Bake for 50–60 minutes, or until a knife slides through easily, then remove the tray or pan from the oven and leave the cauliflower to cool and set for 10 minutes.

5. Cut open and serve with the mango chutney and a little chopped fresh mint and coriander.

crispy fried rice noodles with Chinese spice sprinkle

FOR THE NOODLES
vegetable oil, for deep-frying (see note about contamination on page 8)
100g GF flat rice noodles

FOR THE SPICE SPRINKLE
1 teaspoon sweet paprika
½ teaspoon GF Chinese five spice
½ teaspoon garlic powder
½ teaspoon salt
¼ teaspoon dried chilli flakes
¼ teaspoon cracked black pepper

I love to eat these as a snack, especially just out of the fryer. It's fun to watch the noodles curl up as they cook. Try them with the spice sprinkles on page 244 for other flavours. It's the new popcorn!

Serves 4 · **PREP TIME** *10 minutes* · **COOKING TIME** *15 minutes*

1. Fill a deep-sided pan one-third with oil and heat to 180°C, or use a deep-fat fryer.

2. Combine all the ingredients for the spice sprinkle.

3. Fry the noodles in small batches (about 25g). If you're using noodles that come in a bundle, break them up first into smaller pieces. Drain really well on kitchen paper.

4. Sprinkle over the spice mix while the noodles are still hot and toss well to coat.

ham-wrapped stuffed medjool dates with chorizo

This is another cracking combination. The spicy, sweet caramel flavour, soft, dense texture and buttery paprika and ham juices all work together perfectly. Make sure you crisp up the chorizo slightly for added flavour.

1 medium cooking chorizo
16 medjool dates, stoned but not cut open fully
16 slices of air-dried ham
2 tablespoons vegetable oil

Serves 6–8 • **PREP TIME** *20 minutes* • **COOKING TIME** *20 minutes*

1. Heat a small frying pan.

2. Cut the chorizo into 16 strips the same length as the dates and 5mm thick. Fry the chorizo gently in the pan until crisp. Remove and set aside to cool.

3. Place a strip of chorizo inside each date.

4. Lay a slice of ham on a chopping board. Place the date at one end and roll up the ham so that the date is wrapped one and a half times. You may only need half the slice of ham. Repeat until all the dates are wrapped.

5. When ready to eat, heat the oil in a non-stick frying pan over a low heat and cook the wrapped dates gently for 2–3 minutes, then turn them over and cook for a further 2–3 minutes. Serve warm.

my baked beans

This recipe doesn't really need any introduction. Most people like baked beans; my kids certainly like this version. All pulses, fresh, dried or tinned are really good for you, providing a great source of protein and carbohydrate.

250g pancetta, chopped into 5mm pieces
2 small red onions, peeled and finely chopped
4 garlic cloves, finely chopped
250g dried butterbeans, soaked overnight
400g tin chopped tomatoes
1 x 10g GF vegetable stock cube
1 small red pepper, deseeded and chopped into 1cm pieces
3 tablespoons tomato purée
2 tablespoons cider vinegar
4 tablespoons soft brown sugar
ground black pepper
soured cream, to serve (optional)

Serves 4 · **PREP TIME** *20 minutes* · **COOKING TIME** *1 hour 30 minutes*

1. Heat a medium saucepan and cook the pancetta pieces for 5–6 minutes. Add the onions and garlic, and cook for a further 5–6 minutes.

2. Rinse the soaked beans thoroughly and add them to the pan with the tomatoes, stock cube, red pepper, tomato purée, vinegar and sugar. Season with pepper and bring to a simmer.

3. Stir well, cover and cook for 50–60 minutes. You may need to add a touch of water during the cooking to keep the mixture moist.

4. Once cooked, the mixture will be thick, glossy and smell wonderful. I serve these beans on their own or with a dollop of soured cream.

TIP *You can also cook this dish in the oven preheated to 180°C/gas mark 4. Just pop the pan into the oven once all the ingredients are well mixed.*

red pepper fondant

This makes a change from the roasted peppers we tend to see all too much of these days, plus it doubles up as a delicious dip-cum-spread.

8g leaf gelatine

6 ripe plum tomatoes, halved

2 medium red peppers, quartered and deseeded

2 garlic cloves, peeled and kept whole

1 small onion, peeled and chopped

2 pinches of sugar

4 tablespoons extra virgin olive oil

2 tablespoons white wine vinegar

salt and ground black pepper

200g crème fraîche

8 basil leaves, roughly chopped

GF rice crackers or breadsticks, to serve

Serves 4 · **PREP TIME** *30 minutes* · **COOKING TIME** *45 minutes*

1. Preheat the oven to 230°C/220°C fan/gas mark 8.

2. Soak the gelatine leaves in cold water until soft and pliable.

3. Put the tomatoes, red peppers, garlic, onion, sugar, olive oil, vinegar, and a generous seasoning of salt and pepper into a baking tray. Mix it all up, cover with foil, and heat on the hob until you can hear the contents bubbling.

4. Transfer to the oven and cook for 30 minutes, then remove the foil and return to the oven for a further 15 minutes so that any excess moisture is evaporated.

5. Carefully transfer to a liquidiser and blitz until very smooth, adding a touch of cold water if the mixture is too thick.

6. Spoon the hot purée into a bowl and stir in the softened gelatine until dissolved, then add the crème fraîche and mix well. Finally, stir in the basil and season again if needed. Cover and place in the fridge to set.

7. Serve, spooned onto rice crackers or gluten-free breadsticks.

home-made hummus

I was very lucky some years ago to make four films in Israel. The food, country and people were truly amazing. I cooked all over, from the Dead Sea to Jaffa, home of the eponymous orange. At the Ali Karavan restaurant in Jaffa I tasted three very different types of hummus that were all delicious; it's all they sell. It was not until I tasted the real deal that I realised how far off the mark much of what we have is. Here is my version of what I learnt in Israel. Oh, and serve warm.

350g dried chickpeas
4 teaspoons bicarbonate
   of soda
4–6 tablespoons tahini,
   plus extra to serve
6 garlic cloves, crushed
salt and ground black pepper
juice of 1 large lemon
a dash of olive oil

Serves 8 · **PREP TIME** *15 minutes, plus overnight soaking* · **COOKING TIME** *20–30 minutes*

1. The day before you want to cook, wash the chickpeas well and cover them with cold water. Add 2 teaspoons of the bicarbonate of soda and mix well. Leave in the fridge to soak overnight.

2. The next day, rinse the chickpeas well and place them in a saucepan. Add the remaining 2 teaspoons of bicarbonate of soda, mix well and cover with 2–3cm of water. Bring to the boil, skim well and reduce the heat, then simmer for 20–30 minutes, or until the chickpeas are cooked and soft, but not falling apart. Drain well, reserving the liquid.

3. Put three-quarters of the cooked chickpeas, the tahini and garlic into a food-processor and blitz on full speed for 2 minutes. You may need to add a little of the cooking liquid to loosen the mixture.

4. Spoon the hummus into a bowl and season with salt, pepper and the lemon juice, and mix well. Taste and adjust the seasoning if needed; this is all about personal taste.

5. Serve warm or at room temperature with a swirl of tahini, a dash of olive oil and a few of the warm reserved chickpeas.

TRY THIS *I also like to sprinkle my hummus with lots of chopped fresh parsley or coriander, or even a sprinkling of chopped spring onions and a few slices of green chilli. A little Greek yogurt is also a nice addition.*

red hot chilli popcorn

This spicy popcorn isn't for the faint-hearted, but it is very moreish.

2 tablespoons olive oil

1 level tablespoon dried chilli
   with seeds

250g popping corn

1 tablespoon brown sugar

2 teaspoons smoked paprika

2 tablespoons roughly
   chopped fresh coriander

salt

Serves 4–6 • **PREP TIME** *15 minutes* • **COOKING TIME** *10 minutes*

1. Heat the oil in a heavy-based saucepan over a medium heat, taking care not to burn it. Add the chilli and cook for 10 seconds, then add the corn and stir well. Cover the pan and leave to pop, shaking the pan every now and then. The trick is to listen, and when the popping slows right down (after about 8–10 minutes), remove the pan from the heat.

2. Sprinkle over the sugar, paprika, coriander and a little salt, stir well and serve.

maple syrup black pepper popcorn

This is another nice way of serving popcorn.

---

2 tablespoons olive oil
250g popping corn
3 tablespoons maple syrup
salt and ground black pepper
icing sugar, to serve

TIP *Popcorn keeps well for a couple of days stored in an airtight container.*

Serves 4–6 • **PREP TIME** *15 minutes* • **COOKING TIME** *10 minutes*

1. Heat the oil in a heavy-based saucepan over a medium heat, taking care not to burn it. Add the corn and stir well. Cover the pan and leave to pop, shaking the pan every now and then. The trick is to listen, and when the popping slows right down (after about 8–10 minutes), remove the pan from the heat.

2. Remove the lid, spoon over the maple syrup and sprinkle with salt and pepper, stir well and serve dusted with a little icing sugar.

salted caramel popcorn

I find salted microwave popcorn the easiest, most foolproof way to get the best result for this recipe.

100g packet GF salted microwave popcorn
100g caster sugar
1 tablespoon lemon juice
50g unsalted butter

Serves 4 • **PREP TIME** *5 minutes* • **COOKING TIME** *5–10 minutes*

1. Cook the popcorn according to the packet instructions and tip into a large bowl. Discard any hard kernels.

2. Spread the sugar over the base of a wide, heavy-based saucepan and add enough cold water to cover the sugar, along with the lemon juice. Set the pan over medium heat to melt and caramelise the sugar, swirling the pan until you have an even, dark-golden liquid. Keep a close eye on it and take the pan off the heat before the caramel gets too dark or it will taste bitter. Carefully whisk in 4–5 tablespoons of cold water and the butter until you have a smooth, rich butterscotch.

3. Trickle the butterscotch over the popped popcorn, using two forks to pull the clumps apart and coat the popcorn as it cools.

TIP *If you don't have a microwave, heat 1 tablespoon of oil in a large pan and add 100g popping corn. Cover firmly with a lid and heat gently, shaking the pan until all the corn is popped. The trick is to listen, and when the popping slows right down (after about 8–10 minutes), remove the pan from the heat.*

spiced coconut idli

It was the Chinese who first introduced these steamed snacks to India, many centuries ago. My local Indian takeaway owner, Azad Rahman, once made these for me and they were superb! They just had to go into the book. There is also a sweet version opposite.

50g GF white rice flour
50g ground rice
30g desiccated coconut
3 tablespoons vegetable oil,
   plus extra for greasing
about 200ml cold water or milk
1 teaspoon fenugreek
1 teaspoon ground turmeric
¼ teaspoon dried chilli flakes
1 teaspoon black onion seeds
1 teaspoon mustard seeds
½ small onion, very finely
   chopped
2 garlic cloves, chopped
salt and ground black pepper
½ teaspoon GF baking powder

Makes 16–18 • **PREP TIME** *15 minutes* • **COOKING TIME** *18–20 minutes*

1. Place the rice flour, ground rice and coconut into a bowl and mix well. Add 1 tablespoon of the oil and enough cold water or milk so that you have a wet pouring consistency. Cover with cling film and leave to thicken in the fridge overnight.

2. The next day, oil some idli tins or egg cups. Prepare a steamer.

3. Heat the remaining 2 tablespoons of oil in a frying pan over a low heat and gently fry the spices for 1–2 minutes. Add the onion and garlic, and cook for a couple of minutes to soften, then take off the heat to cool slightly.

4. Add enough cold water or milk to the rested batter until you have the consistency of thick cream, then add the spices, onion, garlic and baking powder. Mix and season well with salt and pepper.

5. Fill the oiled tins or egg cups with the mixture and place them into the steamer for about 20 minutes. The idli will rise and puff up nicely. It's easy to undercook them so when you think they're ready, leave them in for another 5 minutes to be sure.

6. Remove the cooked idli from the steamer and leave for 10 minutes to set. Run a knife around the sides of the tins or cups to release them. A sharp tap and they should come out.

sweet coconut idli

I was lucky enough to film in India some years ago and had these for breakfast most days. They can also be cooked, cooled and deep-fried.

50g GF white rice flour
50g ground rice
30g desiccated coconut
50g caster or granulated sugar
1 tablespoon vegetable oil,
   plus extra for greasing
about 200ml cold water or milk
½ teaspoon GF baking powder
salt and ground black pepper
ice cream, to serve

Serves 16–18 • **PREP TIME** *10 minutes* • **COOKING TIME** *18–20 minutes*

1. Place the rice flour, ground rice, coconut and sugar into a bowl and mix well. Add the oil and enough cold water or milk so that you have a wet pouring consistency. Cover with cling film and leave to thicken in the fridge overnight.

2. The next day, oil some idli tins or egg cups. Prepare a steamer.

3. Add enough cold water or milk to the rested batter until you have the consistency of thick cream, then whisk in the baking powder.

4. Fill the oiled tins or egg cups with the mixture and place them into the steamer for about 20 minutes. The idli will rise and puff up nicely. It's easy to undercook them so when you think they're ready, leave them in for another 5 minutes to be sure.

5. Remove the cooked idli from the steamer and leave for 10 minutes to set. Run a knife around the sides of the tins or cups to release them. A sharp tap and they should come out. Serve with a little gluten-free ice cream.

chunky sweet potato & apple broth

4 tablespoons extra virgin
  olive oil
2 medium onions, finely
  chopped
4 garlic cloves, chopped
1.4kg sweet potatoes (about
  4 medium), peeled and
  chopped fairly small
4 medium potatoes, peeled
  and chopped fairly small
2 Bramley or other cooking
  apples, peeled, cored and
  roughly chopped
2 x 10g GF vegetable stock
  cubes
salt and ground black pepper
200ml double cream
4 heaped tablespoons GF
  mango chutney or relish

This easy to make soup freezes well so it can be made in advance.

Serves 4–6 · **PREP TIME** *30 minutes* · **COOKING TIME** *50 minutes*

1. Heat the oil in a pan over a medium heat and cook the onions and garlic for
5 minutes. Add the potatoes, apples and stock cubes. Pour over 2 litres of cold water,
or enough to just cover, and bring to the boil. Season well with salt and pepper, then
turn down the heat and simmer for 35–40 minutes.

2. Once the potatoes are cooked and very soft, mash roughly with a potato masher
until you have a thickish, chunky purée.

3. Add the cream and chutney or relish. Check the seasoning and adjust if needed.

TIP *This soup freezes well without the cream. When you want to serve it simply defrost,
boil and then add the cream.*

white onion thyme & cider soup

When I worked in the West Country, this soup was a real favourite.
It's very simple but straight to the point. The flavours work really
well together.

50g unsalted butter
4 large white onions, finely
  chopped
4 garlic cloves, roughly
  chopped
½ teaspoon dried thyme
200ml dry cider
2 x 10g GF vegetable stock
  cubes
100ml double cream (optional)
salt and ground black pepper

Serves 4 · **PREP TIME** *15 minutes* · **COOKING TIME** *45 minutes*

1. Heat the butter in a pan over a medium heat and cook the onions, garlic and
thyme for about 10 minutes until softened. Add the cider, stock cubes and enough
cold water to cover the onions by 2–3cm. Bring back to the boil and simmer for
10 minutes, or until the onions are cooked through.

2. Transfer to a liquidiser and blend until very smooth. You may need to do this
in batches.

3. Add the cream, if using, season well with salt and pepper, and serve.

easy pea, potato, spinach & basil soup

This is a brilliant green soup that's packed full of flavour and colour.

2 onions, finely chopped
2 small leeks, finely chopped
2 large potatoes, peeled and
  cubed
2 x 10g GF vegetable stock
  cubes
1 small bunch of fresh basil
200g frozen peas
50–100g fresh spinach leaves
salt and ground black pepper
4 tablespoons extra virgin
  olive oil

Serves 4 · **PREP TIME** *5 minutes* · **COOKING TIME** *20 minutes*

1. Place the onions, leeks, potatoes, stock cubes and basil into a pan. Add enough cold water to cover the vegetables by 3–4cm. Bring to the boil, turn down the heat and simmer gently for about 10 minutes until the potatoes are tender. Add the peas and cook for a further 2 minutes until tender.

2. Spoon into a liquidiser and blitz until smooth. You may need to do this in batches. Add the spinach with the last batch and purée until very smooth.

3. Season with salt and pepper and serve straight away, with a swirl of olive oil on top.

TIP *If you want to save the soup for later, leave the cooked potatoes to cool completely, then purée them with the basil and spinach. This will ensure you have a brilliant-green soup that keeps its colour.*

roast potato, leek & chestnut broth

The key to this broth is really crunchy, tasty potatoes. Boil them really well first so that they're just falling apart, then roast or fry them until they're slightly overcooked and really crisp. Make sure you scrape down and use all the little bits left in the tray or pan at the end.

600g potatoes

8–10 tablespoons vegetable oil

2 large onions, finely chopped

1 large leek, washed and finely
    chopped

4 garlic cloves, chopped

2 x 10g GF vegetable stock
    cubes

200g vacuum-packed
    chestnuts

salt and ground black pepper

4 tablespoons chopped fresh
    parsley

Serves 6–8 • **PREP TIME** *20 minutes* • **COOKING TIME** *30 minutes*

1. Preheat the oven to 220°C/200°C fan/gas mark 7.

2. Put the potatoes into a pan and cover with cold water. Bring to the boil and simmer until really well cooked and just falling apart. Drain well.

3. Heat 6–8 tablespoons of the oil in a roasting tray over a high heat, add the boiled potatoes and, once they're nice and sizzling, pop the tray in the oven and roast for 15–20 minutes until slightly overcooked and really crisp.

4. Meanwhile, heat the remaining 2 tablespoons of oil in a frying pan over a medium heat and cook the onions, leek and garlic for 15 minutes.

5. Add the cooked potatoes to the onions and leek and mix really well. Cover with water, add the stock cubes and bring to the boil.

6. Add the chestnuts and simmer for about 15 minutes, until all the vegetables are cooked. Remove from the heat.

7. Use a potato masher to lightly crush the vegetables in the pan. Season with salt and pepper, stir in the parsley and serve.

TIP *You can make this broth a day ahead and reheat it. It also freezes well. This is a good way to use up leftover potatoes from Sunday lunch.*

Burmese sweet potato curry

I once had a version of this simple dish from a takeaway and it was so good. I sometimes add dried shrimp powder right at the end to give it some kick.

2 tablespoons vegetable oil

1 small onion or 4 shallots, finely chopped

2 tablespoons finely chopped fresh ginger

4 garlic cloves, finely chopped

½ teaspoon dried chilli flakes

½ teaspoon ground turmeric

600g sweet potatoes, peeled and cut into 3cm cubes

2 tablespoons tamarind paste

1 tablespoon ngan pyar yay Burmese fish sauce or nam pla (optional)

salt and ground black pepper

2 tablespoons chopped fresh coriander

2 tablespoons chopped fresh mint leaves

Serves 4 · **PREP TIME** *25 minutes* · **COOKING TIME** *25 minutes*

1. Heat the oil in a large pan. Add the onion or shallots, ginger, garlic, chilli and turmeric, and cook for 5 minutes until softened and lightly browned.

2. Add the sweet potatoes, tamarind, fish sauce and about 150ml of cold water and bring to the boil, then turn down the heat to low, cover and simmer gently for 15–20 minutes, stirring occasionally, until the sweet potato is cooked but not falling apart, and the sauce has thickened.

3. Season with salt and pepper, stir in the coriander and mint and serve straight away.

TRY THIS *You can buy shrimp powder from Asian shops and they add a delicious fish flavour to this dish. Just soak some in a little warm water and lime juice for 20 minutes, drain well and blitz in a food-processor.*

my easy four-pulse dal

100g yellow split peas
100g red lentils
75g green lentils
75g mung beans
3 teaspoons bicarbonate
   of soda
1 tablespoon tomato paste
½ teaspoon GF asafoetida
5 or 6 curry leaves (optional)
6 tablespoons vegetable oil
1 small onion, finely chopped
½ small green chilli, finely
   chopped
50–60g fresh ginger, peeled
   and cut into very thin strips
4 garlic cloves
1 teaspoon cumin seeds
1 teaspoon ground turmeric
6 green cardamom pods,
   crushed
1 teaspoon GF garam masala,
   plus extra to serve
1 teaspoon fenugreek
salt and ground black pepper
2 tablespoons butter
4 tablespoons thick natural
   yogurt
2 tablespoons chopped fresh
   coriander

This recipe is based on two things: one, a trip to Delhi, where I ate many, many different varieties of dal; two, chatting and cooking with my good friend and fabulous Indian chef and restaurateur, Reza Mahammad. I can't get enough dal and would quite happily eat it several times a week. It comes in many forms, with myriad ingredients, so I've tried to keep this one as simple as possible. Asafoetida is not always gluten-free, so check the label. If you can't find it, don't worry; it adds a rounded flavour to the finished dish, but it's not essential.

Serves 4–6 • **PREP TIME** *30 minutes, plus overnight soaking* • **COOKING TIME** *40 minutes*

1. Wash all the pulses thoroughly in cold water, then pop them in a bowl and cover with cold water. Add the bicarbonate of soda and stir well, then cover and refrigerate overnight.

2. The next day, rinse the pulses really well and tip them into a clean pan. Pour over enough cold water so that they're just covered and bring to the boil. Skim well, turn down the heat and add the tomato paste, asafoetida and curry leaves, if using. Simmer gently for 40–50 minutes. You may need to top up with boiling water.

3. Meanwhile, heat 2 tablespoons of the oil in a frying pan over a medium heat and cook the onion, chilli and ginger until really well browned, then add the garlic, reduce the heat and cook for a further 10–15 minutes. Spoon into a bowl and wipe the pan with kitchen paper.

4. Add the remaining 4 tablespoons of oil to the pan and cook the cumin, turmeric, cardamom, garam masala and fenugreek over a gentle heat, to take a little colour and release the lovely aromas. Spoon over the onion mixture.

5. Once the pulses are cooked, the mixture will start to thicken and look more like stew, this is perfect. Season well with salt and a little pepper.

6. Stir in the onion and spice mixture and mix well, test for seasoning and adjust as needed.

7. Just before serving, stir in the butter and top with few blobs of thick yogurt, plenty of chopped fresh coriander and a sprinkling of gluten-free garam masala.

braised kidney bean & tomato curry

Great as an accompaniment to meat or fish, or with rice crackers.

Serves 4 • **PREP TIME** *15 minutes* • **COOKING TIME** *35–40 minutes*

FOR THE SAUCE

2 ripe tomatoes

4 tablespoons tomato purée

1 x 10g GF vegetable stock cube

¼ teaspoon dried chilli

a pinch of salt

FOR THE BEANS

2 tablespoons vegetable oil

2 large onions, finely chopped

4 garlic cloves

1 tablespoon GF Madras curry paste

2 x 400g tins red kidney beans, drained well

salt and ground black pepper

1. Place all the ingredients for the sauce into a liquidiser and blend until really smooth. You may have to add a little cold water to loosen the mixture.

2. Meanwhile heat the oil in a frying pan over a high heat and cook the onions and garlic for a few minutes until browned. Add the curry paste and continue to cook for 2 minutes. Add the drained beans and warm through.

3. Add the sauce to the vegetables and bring to the boil. Season well with salt and pepper, turn down the heat and simmer for 15 minutes then serve.

spinach & potato empanadas

Potato, spinach and onions is a great combination.

Serves 4 • **PREP TIME** *15 minutes* • **COOKING TIME** *12–15 minutes in batches*

1 x quantity Empanada Dough (page 151)

1 large potato, peeled and cut into 5mm cubes

4 tablespoons extra virgin olive oil

1 small onion, finely chopped

2 small garlic cloves, finely chopped

125g fresh spinach

salt and ground black pepper

1 egg, beaten

vegetable oil, for deep-frying (see note about contamination on page 8)

1. Bring a pan of water to the boil and cook the potato until soft but not broken up. Strain well and cover with cling film.

2. Heat the olive oil in a frying pan over a low heat and cook the onion and garlic for about 10 minutes to soften really well. Add the spinach and cook down until fully wilted. Add the cooked potato and season well with salt and pepper.

3. Heat a deep-fryer or deep-sided pan one-third filled with oil to 180°C.

4. Roll out the dough with a dusting of gluten-free flour. Use a 6cm cutter to cut out circles, then brush the edges with a little beaten egg. Fill one side, then fold over the dough and press well. Press the edge with a fork to get a nicer seal and appearance.

5. Deep-fry for 2–3 minutes until blistered and cooked through, turning occasionally to colour evenly.

chickpea & cumin pancakes with tomatoes, red onion & coriander

I've served these simple but really tasty pancakes with spicy mango chutney and thick yogurt, but they're also good with tomato salsa.

2 ripe plum tomatoes

1 small red onion, very finely chopped

1–2 pinches of dried red chilli flakes

1 teaspoon very finely chopped fresh ginger

a pinch of GF garam masala, plus extra to garnish

½ teaspoon ground cumin

4 tablespoons olive oil

a pinch of xanthan gum

½ teaspoon GF baking powder

150g GF gram flour

2 tablespoons chopped fresh coriander, plus a few leaves to garnish

salt and ground black pepper

4 tablespoons GF spicy mango chutney

4 tablespoons thick yogurt

Makes 8 small pancakes • **PREP TIME** *15 minutes* • **COOKING TIME** *6–8 minutes*

1. Put the tomatoes, onion, chilli flakes, ginger, garam masala, cumin and 2 tablespoons of the oil into a liquidiser and blitz to a thick paste.

2. In a small bowl, mix together the xanthan gum, baking powder and flour, then add the coriander and season with salt and pepper. Pour in the spicy tomato paste and mix well (the mixture will tighten slightly as the gum starts to work).

3. Heat the remaining 2 tablespoons of oil in a non-stick frying pan over a medium heat. Spoon a ladleful of batter into the pan and cook for 2–3 minutes. Carefully flip over and cook for a further 2 minutes to just set. Repeat to make eight small pancakes.

4. Serve warm with a spoonful of mango chutney and a dollop of yogurt. Garnish with a few coriander leaves and a sprinkling of gluten-free garam masala.

simple Singapore noodles

Another quick and easy dish that's really simple to prepare. It will serve two as a main, or four as a starter. It's pretty much a whole meal at once, and not only tasty but also very filling.

1 medium potato
250g GF rice noodles
4–6 tablespoons olive oil
2 medium eggs, beaten
150g bean curd, drained and
    cut into small cubes
6 tablespoons GF tomato
    ketchup
2 tablespoons GF sweet
    chilli sauce
4 tablespoons GF tamari sauce
2 tablespoons sliced spring
    onions, plus extra to garnish
2 red chillies, finely sliced
4 tablespoons chopped
    Thai basil
salt and ground black pepper

Serves 2 as a starter, or 4 as a main • **PREP TIME** *15 minutes* • **COOKING TIME** *10 minutes*

1. Bring a pan of water to the boil and cook the potato until tender. Remove with a slotted spoon and roughly chop. Add the noodles to the pan and cook according to the packet instructions.

2. Meanwhile, heat the oil in a large wok or frying pan over a high heat. Add the eggs and make a large thin omelette. Once cooked, slide onto a board and roll up.

3. Add the cooked potato to the hot wok and warm through for 2–3 minutes, then add the bean curd and warm through. Add the ketchup, chilli sauce, tamari and spring onions, and mix well. Add the noodles and warm through gently. Finally, thinly slice the omelette and at it to the pan. Gently mix everything together.

4. Divide between warm bowls and garnish with the spring onions, chillies and Thai basil.

Korean tofu hotpot

400g silken or very soft tofu
500ml boiling water
2 x 10g GF beef stock cubes
4 tablespoons rice wine
   vinegar
4 garlic cloves, finely chopped
1 tablespoon very finely
   chopped red chilli
1 tablespoon sesame oil
8 spring onions, finely sliced
   on the diagonal
2 tablespoons GF tamari sauce
2 teaspoons brown sugar
2 tablespoons vegetable oil
boiled or steamed rice,
   to serve (optional)

Koreans would make this soup using gochujang, a fiery, fragrant chilli paste made with malted barley, rice flour and red pepper powder. However, as it contains malted barley, it is not suitable for people with coeliac disease. There really isn't an authentic alternative, so I've created a simple version of this classic Korean soup.

Serves 4 · **PREP TIME** *15 minutes* · **COOKING TIME** *15 minutes*

1. Drain the tofu well on kitchen paper and cut into 2cm cubes. Pat dry.

2. Place the boiling water, stock cubes and vinegar in a pan, and bring to the boil. Once the stock cubes are dissolved add the garlic, chilli, sesame oil and spring onions. Reduce the heat to a simmer and cook for 2 minutes. Add the tamari and sugar.

3. Heat the oil in a large frying pan over a medium heat. Lightly brown the tofu, then spoon it into the hot broth. Check the seasoning.

4. Serve in small, deep bowls with plain boiled or steamed rice, if you like.

TRY THIS *Try substituting some finely sliced chicken, beef or pork for the tofu. I sometimes add prawns, too.*

roasted vegetables with salse verde

I love the bright colours and textures in this delicious dish. It makes a filling main meal but can also be a fantastic addition as a side dish.

350g yellow, red and orange
   peppers
1 small carrot
1 large red onion, peeled
1 medium courgette
2 garlic cloves
2 tablespoons olive oil
a bunch of fresh basil leaves,
   sliced
ground black pepper

FOR THE CHILLI AND HERB PASTE
1 small green chilli, deseeded
   and finely chopped
a small handful of fresh flat-
   leaf parsley, leaves picked
   and finely chopped
a small handful of basil, finely
   chopped
1 tablespoon olive oil
1 teaspoon lemon juice

FOR THE YOGURT DRESSING
1 tablespoon plain yogurt
   per person
a squeeze of lemon juice
a few mint leaves, finely
   chopped

Serves 2 as a main, or 4 as a side · **PREP TIME** *10 minutes* · **COOKING TIME** *35 minutes*

1. Preheat the oven to 220°C/200°C fan/gas mark 7.

2. Trim the vegetables and cut them into similarly sized chunks, then spread them out in a large roasting dish. Add the whole, unpeeled cloves of garlic and the olive oil and turn the vegetables to coat.

3. Roast for 30–40 minutes, turning the vegetables halfway through, until beginning to colour at the edges.

4. Meanwhile, mix together the ingredients for the paste and pound them to a rough paste. A pestle and mortar is best for this, but chopping the ingredients very finely by hand is also fine.

5. Thin down the yogurt for the dressing with a little lemon juice and stir in the chopped mint.

6. Remove the tray from the oven and season the cooked vegetables with pepper. Once cool, squeeze the roasted garlic from the skins, chop and mix back into the roasted vegetables with the basil. Stir through the yogurt dressing so that you can still see all the bright colours of the vegetables.

7. Pile the vegetables onto serving plates, spoon over a tablespoon of the herb paste and serve.

leek & Gruyère quiche

The leek and Gruyère in this dish work well together with a little added nutmeg. I add crushed gluten-free cornflakes to the pastry for extra bite and a few on the top of the quiche for texture. It sounds odd but it works well. You don't need to bake the pastry blind; the sides are strengthened and sealed with an egg glaze before cooking.

Makes one 23cm tart to serve 6–8 • **PREP TIME** *35 minutes* • **COOKING TIME** *1 hour*

FOR THE BASE

140g GF Sorghum Flour Blend (page 14), plus extra for dusting

50g GF cornflakes, finely crushed

½ level teaspoon xanthan gum

a pinch of salt

90g margarine, straight from the fridge

40g thick yogurt or soured cream

1 tablespoon white wine vinegar

1 medium egg yolk, plus 1 beaten egg

FOR THE FILLING

300ml milk

2–3 tablespoons vegetable oil

2 medium leeks, washed and very finely chopped

2 garlic cloves

2 tablespoons roughly chopped parsley

150g Gruyère cheese, grated or cut into small cubes

2 medium eggs

½ teaspoon grated nutmeg

salt and ground black pepper

40g GF cornflakes, finely crushed

1. First make the pastry base. Preheat the oven to 200°C/190°C/gas mark 6.

2. Put the flour, cornflakes, xanthan gum and salt into a food-processor with the margarine and pulse until you have a fine crumb mixture.

3. In a separate bowl, mix together the yogurt or soured cream, vinegar and egg yolk with 2 tablespoons of water. Add to the flour and margarine mixture, and pulse together well. Remove and knead gently, then chill for 20 minutes.

4. Roll out on a lightly floured surface, then roll onto the rolling pin and line a 23cm tart tin. Prick the base with a fork and bake for 25 minutes to set, then remove from the oven and brush with the beaten egg to seal really well. Use all the egg as gluten-free pastry can be fragile. Return to the oven for 5 minutes to set the egg, then remove and set aside. Reduce the heat to 180°C/gas mark 4.

5. Now make the filling. Put the milk in a pan over a high heat, bring to the boil then cool for 10 minutes.

6. Meanwhile, heat the oil in a frying pan over a medium heat and cook the leeks and garlic for 10 minutes. Once softened, strain well to remove any excess moisture, then spread over the base of the cooked pastry base. Sprinkle over the parsley and top with the cheese.

7. Place the quiche on a baking tray. Beat the eggs with the warm milk and nutmeg, and season with salt and pepper. Pour over the cheese to fill the tart. Sprinkle over the crushed cornflakes.

8. Bake for 25–30 minutes until set but with a slight wobble in the centre. Cool slightly before cutting and serving.

roasted pumpkin & sage risotto

The thing to remember with this colourful risotto is to roast the pumpkin or squash really well to increase the flavour. Also leave to rest for 3–4 minutes before eating to give the cheese and butter time to melt. If you want to do something special, hollow out a large pumpkin, or four small ones, and serve the risotto inside.

Serves 4 · **PREP TIME** *30 minutes* · **COOKING TIME** *25–30 minutes*

500g pumpkin or squash (from about 1kg whole vegetables), peeled and deseeded then roughly chopped
2 tablespoons olive oil
1 small onion, very finely chopped
1 garlic clove, very finely chopped
180g risotto rice
100ml medium white wine (optional)
800ml hot GF vegetable stock
1 tablespoon chopped fresh sage
50–75g butter
50–75g Parmesan-style hard cheese, finely grated
salt and ground black pepper

1. Preheat the oven to 220°C/200°C/gas mark 7 and roast the pumpkin or squash until soft. Leave to cool slightly, then chop into 1cm cubes.

2. Heat the oil in a pan over a medium heat and soften the onion for 1–2 minutes. Add the garlic and mix well.

3. Add the rice to the pan and coat in the oil and onion mixture. Add the white wine, if using, and cook until almost evaporated, stirring constantly, then add a couple of ladlefuls of stock and bring to the boil.

4. Turn down the heat slightly and add the sage. Keep adding spoonfuls of stock until the rice is cooked and creamy, but not overcooked. It should be al dente.

5. At this stage, add the pumpkin, butter and cheese, and mix through, seasoning well with salt and pepper. Cover, remove from the heat and leave to rest for 2–3 minutes.

6. Serve in hollowed-out warm pumpkins or in deep bowls with a few Parmesan shavings on top.

roasted vegetable pizza sauce

1 red pepper, deseeded and
   cut into small chunks
1 yellow pepper, deseeded and
   cut into small chunks
1 small courgette, deseeded
   and cut into small chunks
1 small red onion, deseeded
   and cut into small chunks
2–3 tablespoons olive oil
ground black pepper
1 GF pizza base (page 32)
40g mozzarella, Gruyère or
   Cheddar cheese, grated
fresh basil or oregano,
   to garnish

FOR THE TOMATO SAUCE
1 tablespoon vegetable oil
1 onion, chopped
1 garlic clove, chopped
30g unsalted sun-dried
   tomatoes, soaked
200g tin chopped tomatoes
1 teaspoon red wine or
   balsamic vinegar
a pinch of dark brown sugar

This fresh sauce, with the sweetness of roasted peppers, is perfect for a pizza topping and will be delicious on pasta too. Of course, you can use a jar of pizza tomato sauce for speed, and roasted peppers from the deli, too.

Serves 4 • PREP TIME *20 minutes* • COOKING TIME *45 minutes, plus 10 minutes*

1. Preheat the oven to 220°C/200°C/gas mark 7.

2. Spread out all the vegetables in a large roasting dish lined with foil. Add the oil and turn the vegetables to coat them. Roast for about 30 minutes, turning them halfway through, until beginning to colour at the edges. Remove from the oven and season with pepper.

3. Meanwhile, heat the oil for the tomato sauce in a pan over a medium heat and fry the onion and garlic for about 5 minutes until golden. Stir in the remaining sauce ingredients and cook for a further 20 minutes on a low heat until the sauce has thickened.

4. Spread the pizza base with the tomato sauce. Lay the roasted vegetables over the top, and scatter over the grated cheese. Bake for 10 minutes until bubbling. Serve straight away, scattered with fresh basil or oregano leaves.

TIP *For a non-vegetarian option, top with a few slices of chorizo.*

lasagnette with asparagus, tomatoes & shallots

Lasagnette is a ribbon pasta that's like a thinner version of lasagne sheets, with attractive fluted edges. I once had it for lunch in Capri, but I haven't seen it since, so I've created my own version.

400g GF Rich Pasta Dough
  (page 39)
GF flour, for dusting
4 tablespoons olive oil
4 shallots or 1 large onion,
  finely chopped
4 garlic cloves, chopped
2 tablespoons tomato purée
400g tin chopped tomatoes
1 x 10g GF vegetable stock
  cube
4 tablespoons white wine
  vinegar
1 tablespoon caster sugar
salt and ground black pepper
12 asparagus spears, trimmed
  then grilled, fried or steamed

Serves 4 · **PREP TIME** *25 minutes* · **COOKING TIME** *35–40 minutes*

1. Divide the pasta dough into four equal pieces and roll out as thinly as possible. You may need a little gluten-free flour to help this along. Use a pizza or fluted ravioli pasta wheel, cut out long 3–4cm wide strips. Repeat until you have a pile of fresh pasta ribbons.

2. Bring a large pan of salted water to the boil.

3. Meanwhile, heat the oil in a pan over a low heat and soften the onion or shallots for 5–6 minutes, then add the garlic and cook for a further 10 minutes.

4. Add the tomato purée, tomatoes, stock cube and 100ml of cold water, and bring to a simmer. Cook for 15 minutes or until the sauce has thickened slightly. Add the vinegar and sugar, and season with salt and pepper.

5. Plunge the pasta into the boiling water and cook for 2–3 minutes. Drain really well, then toss in a couple of tablespoons of olive oil to stop it sticking together. Season, if liked.

6. Serve the warm pasta ribbons topped with the rich tomato sauce with the asparagus on top.

TIP *Asparagus can be cooked in various ways, so roll in a little oil and either char grill or gently fry, taking a nice colour and flavour. Or boil or steam lightly, but do not overcook. You could chop and add to the tomato sauce and simmer for a few minutes.*

macaroni 'n' cheese toasties

200g dried GF pasta, such as
  small macaroni
  or penne
3 tablespoons olive oil, plus
  extra for frying
1 onion, finely chopped
275ml milk
½ x 10g GF vegetable stock
  cube
40g butter, softened, plus extra
  for frying
30g GF plain flour
175g strong Cheddar cheese,
  grated
1–2 pinches of grated nutmeg
1 level tablespoon GF English
  mustard
salt and ground black pepper
4 tablespoons chopped fresh
  basil
8 slices of GF white bread

TIP *A nice dollop of pickle or spicy
mango chutney finishes this dish
off perfectly.*

This sandwich is a one-off. The secret is to set it in a loaf tin and
chill it really well, otherwise you've got no chance of cutting it.

Serves 4 • **PREP TIME** *15 minutes* • **COOKING TIME** *20 minutes*

1. Line a small loaf tin with cling film, wetting the tin first (to help the cling film stick).

2. Bring a pan of salted water to the boil and cook the pasta until al dente. Drain well,
stirring in 1 tablespoon of the oil to stop the pasta sticking together. Set aside.

3. Warm the remaining 2 tablespoons of oil in a pan over a medium heat and cook the
onion for 5 minutes until softened. Add the milk and stock cube, and bring to the boil.

4. Meanwhile, in a bowl, mix together the butter and flour to form a paste.

5. Once the milk is boiling, reduce the heat to a simmer and whisk in the butter and
flour roux. Cook for 2 minutes, then take off the heat and stir in 125g of the cheese
and the cooked pasta. Add the nutmeg, mustard, salt, pepper and basil. Spoon into
the loaf tin and press down well. Cover and cool, then chill until completely cold.

6. When fully chilled, turn the pasta brick out onto a chopping board and remove
the cling film. Using a sharp knife, slice 3–4 cm slices.

7. Butter the gluten-free bread and make four sandwiches with the pasta slices,
pressing them together gently to seal. Return to the fridge to chill.

8. Preheat the oven to 200°C/gas mark 6. Heat a little oil and a knob of butter in a large
frying pan over a high heat until just browning. Cook the sandwiches for 2–3 minutes
until lightly browned, then turn them over gently and transfer the pan to the oven.
Cook gently until the pasta is warmed through and the bread nicely browned.

9. Cut into triangles and serve straight away.

Romesco pasta sauce

This is a great pasta sauce, but it's also really good as a dip; delicious served with roasted vegetables and, if you're not vegetarian, grilled fish or roasted meats.

6 tablespoons olive oil
1 red pepper, finely chopped
4 garlic cloves, finely chopped
½ teaspoon dried chilli flakes
100g almonds, skin-on
2–3 tablespoons vinegar,
    preferably sherry vinegar
3 large ripe tomatoes, roughly
    chopped
salt and ground black pepper
4 tablespoons chopped fresh
    parsley

Serves 6–8 · **PREP TIME** *15 minutes* · **COOKING TIME** *15 minutes*

1. Heat the oil in a pan over a medium heat and cook the red pepper for 2–3 minutes until slightly coloured.

2. Transfer to a food-processor with the garlic, chilli, almonds, vinegar, tomatoes, salt, pepper and parsley, and blend to a smooth sauce. You may need to add a little more oil to get a good consistency, it should be the same thickness as double cream.

3. Check the seasoning and adjust if needed.

fettuccine with mushrooms

400g GF Rich Pasta Dough
(page 39), divided into 4
GF flour, for dusting
225ml double cream
200g brown-capped
mushrooms, sliced
4 garlic cloves, chopped
salt and ground black pepper
50g pine nuts, toasted
4 tablespoons chopped fresh
parsley

I sometimes use different varieties of mushrooms or a little Gorgonzola (which isn't vegetarian) to the finished sauce; there are really no hard and fast rules here – it's all about taste and simplicity.

Serves 4 · **PREP TIME** *25 minutes* · **COOKING TIME** *15–20 minutes*

1. Roll out the dough as thinly as possible. Using a pizza or fluted ravioli pasta wheel, cut long 2cm wide strips.

2. In a pan over a medium–low heat, combine the cream, mushrooms and garlic, and simmer for 2 minutes, then season well with salt and pepper, and take off the heat.

3. Cook the fettuccine in boiling water for 2–3 minutes, then drain really well.

4. Add the pine nuts to the cream and mushroom sauce, and stir thoroughly.

5. Spoon the cooked pasta into the creamy sauce with the parsley and mix well. Check the seasoning and adjust if needed. Spoon into deep bowls and serve.

fusilli with tomato & almonds

4 garlic cloves, peeled
150g unblanched almonds
50g pine nuts
15 fresh basil leaves
4 tablespoons chopped
fresh mint
75ml extra virgin olive oil
10 baby plum tomatoes,
quartered
salt and ground black pepper
350g GF fusilli
Parmesan-style hard cheese,
grated, to serve

This hearty dish is very easy to prepare and cook. I really like the texture, the kick of garlic and the milky flavour of the almonds.

Serves 4 · **PREP TIME** *20 minutes* · **COOKING TIME** *15 minutes*

1. Place the garlic, nuts, basil and mint into a food-processor or pestle and mortar and blitz for 2 minutes, or bash to a paste. Add the oil in a thin stream and keep blending. You may need a little more oil to get a thick consistency. Spoon the mixture into a bowl and stir in the tomatoes. Season well with salt and pepper, and set aside to rest.

2. Bring a pan of salted water to the boil and cook the pasta until al dente, drain well and return to the hot, dry pan. Stir through the sauce.

3. Spoon into bowls and serve with the grated cheese.

fish & shellfish

warm mussel watercress & potato flan

Mussels are probably the cheapest shellfish you can buy. Nowadays, most are rope-grown in free-flowing water. This ensures very little grit or sand, though they can still be slightly gritty, so wash them thoroughly. Discard any that remain open when tapped lightly and remove the beards (the threads that attach the mussels to the rope). This flan is best served warm.

100g potatoes, any variety
1kg fresh mussels, debearded and cleaned
250ml whipping cream
½ x 10g GF fish stock cube
25g unsalted butter
1 small onion, finely chopped
a pinch of saffron threads or good-quality saffron powder
1 garlic clove, crushed
24cm GF shortcrust pastry case, baked blind (see pages 40 and 17)
1 small bunch of watercress, chopped
2 tablespoons freshly chopped parsley
salt and ground black pepper
2 medium eggs, plus 2 yolks

4–6 portions • **PREP TIME** *25 minutes* • **COOKING TIME** *45 minutes*

1. Preheat the oven to 180°C/160°C fan/gas mark 4.

2. Put a pan of water over a high heat and bring to the boil. Add the potatoes and cook until tender. Remove with a slotted spoon and cut into small cubes.

3. Tip the mussels into a separate large pan over a high heat with about 100ml of cold water. Put the lid on and cook for 6–8 minutes until all the mussels are opened. Discard any that don't open when tapped. Set aside to cool slightly, then shell all the mussels.

4. Bring the cream to the boil and add the stock cube. Whisk until the stock cube has dissolved.

5. Melt the butter in a frying pan over a medium heat and cook the onion, saffron and garlic until slightly softened. Spoon the mixture into the bottom of the gluten-free pastry case and top with the mussels, watercress and potatoes. Sprinkle over the parsley and season well with salt and pepper.

6. Whisk together the eggs and yolks, and carefully pour over the warm cream, straining the mixture into the pastry case through a sieve.

7. Bake until the flan is just set in the middle, then remove from the oven and set aside for 15 minutes so that the residual heat finishes cooking the flan. Cut and serve.

easy crab chowder

1 x 10g GF fish stock cube
1 x 10g GF chicken stock cube
2 large potatoes, peeled and
  roughly cubed
2 large onions, roughly
  chopped
2 garlic cloves, chopped
200g tin sweetcorn, drained
salt and ground black pepper
200g fine green beans,
  chopped into 1cm pieces
300ml milk
250g fresh crabmeat, picked
4 tablespoons chopped fresh
  parsley, to serve

The secret of any chowder is to make sure the end result is thick with vegetables and packed full of fish, so don't be shy.

Serves 4 · **PREP TIME** *30 minutes* · **COOKING TIME** *45 minutes*

1. Put about 600ml of cold water in a pan over a medium heat. Add the stock cubes, potatoes, onions, garlic and sweetcorn. Season well with salt and pepper, and cook for 30 minutes until the potatoes are cooked and just falling apart.

2. Add the green beans and cook for 5 minutes, then add the milk and crab meat.

3. Serve with plenty of chopped parsley sprinkled on top.

mussel & brown mushroom miso

4 tablespoons GF brown
  miso paste
20g Japanese bonito flakes
1kg fresh mussels, debearded
  and cleaned
150g brown-capped
  mushrooms such as
  chestnuts, finely sliced
salt and ground black pepper
6 small spring onions, sliced
  diagonally

Like a lot of Japanese food, this dish is so easy to prepare but will give you lovely results. This is a simple broth with lots of fresh flavours. Make sure the miso paste you are using is gluten free. Some have added barley and wheat extract.

Serves 4 · **PREP TIME** *15 minutes* · **COOKING TIME** *20 minutes*

1. Put a pan large enough to hold all the mussels over a high heat. Add 600ml of cold water, the miso paste and the Japanese bonito flakes. Bring to the boil and simmer for 2 minutes. Add the mussels and bring back to the boil. Cover with a lid and cook for 10 minutes until all the mussels are opened. Discard any that do not open. Tip the mussels into a colander over a large bowl, retaining the cooking liquor.

2. Let the mussels cool for a minute or so, then carefully remove all the shells.

3. Strain the miso cooking stock through a fine sieve so that you have a smooth liquid. Pour into a clean pan. Add the mushrooms to the pan and bring to the boil, then take off the heat and season well with salt and pepper. Add the mussel meat and spring onions to the pan and stir.

4. Serve straight away in deep bowls.

deep-fried seaweed scallops with tomato & ginger mayonnaise

2 eggs, lightly beaten
180g (about 24) baby scallops
a pinch of salt
a pinch of caster sugar
vegetable oil, for deep-
  frying (see note about
  contamination on page 8)

FOR THE SEAWEED MIX
1 tablespoon finely chopped
  fresh coriander
¼ teaspoon chilli flakes
20g cornflour, arrowroot or
  tapioca starch
10g fine seaweed flakes
a pinch of salt

FOR THE MAYONNAISE
4 heaped tablespoons GF
  mayonnaise
2 tablespoons GF tomato
  ketchup
2 tablespoons chopped fresh
  coriander
1 tablespoon very finely
  chopped fresh ginger
1 tablespoon GF tamari sauce

This is another Japanese-inspired recipe that's very simple to make. I use very fine seaweed flakes that are now available in larger supermarkets.

Serves 4 · **PREP TIME** *25 minutes* · **COOKING TIME** *12–15 minutes*

1. Place all the ingredients for the spice mix into a bowl.

2. Mix together all the ingredients for the mayonnaise.

3. Place the beaten eggs into a separate bowl.

4. Heat the oil to 180°C in a deep-fat fryer or deep-sided pan filled to a third with oil.

5. Dry the scallops on kitchen paper. Dip them into the seaweed mix, then into the beaten egg, then back into the seaweed mix. Coat well, then shake off any excess.

6. Fry in small batches until coloured and crisp. The seaweed coating will go a lovely dark green colour.

7. Drain well on kitchen paper, sprinkle with salt and a little caster sugar, and serve with the ginger mayonnaise.

Singapore chilli crab

This recipe is pretty authentic, even down to the ketchup. I cooked it three times in Singapore: once in a hawker market, once in a smart fish restaurant and once on my own on the harbourside. The only traditional ingredient that's missing from my recipe is the beaten egg that's whisked into the finished sauce. If you want to give it a go, just before you serve, pour in a beaten egg and mix it quickly into the hot crab and sauce. The egg thickens the sauce and gives it a weird threaded egg look. But hey, who am I to question? Once cooked, tuck straight in with your fingers.

4 tablespoons vegetable oil
2 large crabs, each chopped
    into 4, large claws cracked
4 medium red chillies, chopped
4 garlic cloves, crushed
4 tablespoons very finely
    chopped fresh ginger
200ml GF tomato ketchup or
    thick tomato sauce
salt and ground black pepper
sugar, to taste
4 tablespoons chopped spring
    onions, to serve

Serves 2–4 • **PREP TIME** *20 minutes* • **COOKING TIME** *20 minutes*

1. Heat most of the oil in a large wok over a high heat. Add the crab pieces and cook for 5–6 minutes, turning occasionally so that they brown well. Remove from the pan and set aside. You may need to do this in two batches to keep the heat in the wok.

2. Add the remaining oil, then cook the chillies, garlic and ginger for 2–3 minutes to take some colour. Add the ketchup or tomato sauce and bring to the boil.

3. Season to taste with salt and pepper or sugar and add the crab. Cook for a further 4–5 minutes, turning often, until the crab is cooked through. You may need to add a little water.

4. Serve hot and steaming with the spring onions sprinkled over the top.

salt & pepper squid

14–16 baby squid, cleaned
    and dried on kitchen paper
200g GF tapioca flour or
    cornflour
300ml milk
vegetable oil, for deep-
    frying (see note about
    contamination on page 8)

FOR THE SPICE MIX
1 teaspoon dried garlic powder
1 teaspoon GF celery salt
1 teaspoon ground black
    pepper
1 teaspoon caster sugar
½ teaspoon table salt
¼ teaspoon dried chilli flakes

FOR THE DIPPING SAUCE
1 teaspoon shrimp paste
1 small red chilli, finely
    chopped
1 large tablespoon GF
    lemongrass paste
1 tablespoon caster sugar
1 teaspoon finely chopped
    fresh ginger
juice of 2 large limes
4 tablespoons GF tamari sauce
1 tablespoon nam pla fish
    sauce
2 tablespoons chopped fresh
    coriander
2 tablespoons finely chopped
    Thai basil

TO SERVE
lime wedges, to serve
a few fresh red chillies, very
    finely sliced
2–3 tablespoons finely
    shredded Thai basil leaves

This is a very popular dish all around the world. It's so simple but really, really tasty. The smaller the squid the crisper the end result. I find that frozen defrosted squid, if dried well, is excellent for frying. The secret is to fry in oil that is really hot.

Serves 4–6 as a starter • **PREP TIME** *20 minutes* • **COOKING TIME** *3–4 minutes, in small batches*

1. In a small bowl, combine all the ingredients for the spice mix.

2. To make the dipping sauce, mix together the shrimp paste, chilli, lemongrass paste, sugar and ginger. Add the lime juice, tamari and fish sauce, and mix well. Add the herbs.

3. Remove the heads and tentacles from the squid and pat dry. Slice open the bodies and score with a sharp knife. Dust with a little spice mix, a few squid at a time.

4. Prepare two bowls – one with the tapioca or cornflour, the other with the milk. Dip the squid into the flour, then the milk, then back into the flour. Double-dip if necessary.

5. Heat the oil to 190°C in a deep-fat fryer or deep-sided pan filled one-third with oil. Fry the squid in small batches until golden and crisp. Drain on kitchen paper.

6. Sprinkle over a little of the remaining spice mix, a few Thai basil leaves and a few chilli slices, and give the squid a shake. Serve straight away with fresh lime wedges and the dipping sauce.

fried vermicelli noodle prawns with yuzu & a toasted sesame dressing

I really like the taste and texture of fried rice noodles. They also make a nice coating for flash-fried ingredients like fish. Don't worry too much if the noodles don't coat the filling fully as it's the cornflour and egg that seal the fish; the purpose of the vermicelli is to puff slightly for a lovely spiky texture.

Yuzu is an Asian fruit that looks like a yellow tangerine and has a sharp taste similar to lemon. You can buy bottled juice in larger supermarkets and Asian shops. If you can't find it, then a 50:50 mix of satsuma or tangerine juice mixed with lime or lemon juice is okay.

vegetable oil, for deep-frying (see note about contamination on page 8)
75–80g GF fine rice vermicelli
2 tablespoons cornflour, arrowroot or tapioca starch
2 medium eggs, beaten
180g (about 12) freshwater prawns, shelled, intestinal tract removed and dried on kitchen paper

FOR THE DIPPING SAUCE
4 tablespoons yuzu juice
2 teaspoons sesame oil
2 tablespoons mirin
1 tablespoon GF tamari sauce
1 tablespoon very finely chopped fresh ginger

Serves 4 · **PREP TIME** *20 minutes* · **COOKING TIME** *10–12 minutes*

1. Heat the oil to 180°C in a deep-fat fryer or deep-sided pan filled one-third full with oil.

2. In a large bowl, break up the vermicelli into 1–2cm pieces.

3. Put the cornflour in a small bowl and the beaten eggs into a separate bowl.

4. Coat the prawns first in the starch, then the egg, then the vermicelli, pressing them onto the prawns.

5. Fry 5 or 6 prawns at a time for 3–4 minutes until well puffed and a light golden colour. Let the oil get back up to 180°C and cook the rest of the prawns in batches.

6. Meanwhile, combine all the ingredients for the dipping sauce in a bowl and mix together well.

7. Serve the hot prawns with the dipping sauce.

Thai green prawn & oyster curry

4 tablespoons vegetable oil

4 spring onions, chopped

2 tablespoons chopped fresh lemongrass, or 1 tablespoon GF lemongrass paste

1 tablespoon Thai shrimp paste

4 tablespoons GF Thai green curry paste

400ml GF coconut milk

1 tablespoon nam pla fish sauce

500g raw freshwater prawns, shelled

salt and ground black pepper

a pinch of sugar, preferably palm

juice of 1 large lime

4 tablespoons chopped fresh coriander

8 freshly shucked oysters

steamed or boiled rice, to serve

I cooked this after a lesson from the head chef at the Mandarin Oriental Hotel in Bangkok. I use freshwater prawns – the bigger the better – and add fresh oysters at the last minute, so they gently poach.

Serves 4 • **PREP TIME** *20 minutes* • **COOKING TIME** *15 minutes*

1. Heat the oil in a frying pan or wok over a high heat and cook the spring onions for a minute or so to soften. Add the lemongrass, shrimp paste and curry paste, and cook for a further 2–3 minutes.

2. Add the coconut milk and bring to a simmer, then cook for 2–3 minutes to thicken. Add the nam pla and prawns, and cook until just pink, but do not overcook. Remove from the heat, and season well with salt and pepper. Add the sugar, lime juice and coriander.

3. Add the oysters and serve straight away with steamed or boiled rice.

simple spaghetti with capers, parsley anchovies & chilli

4 tablespoons extra virgin olive oil

1 small onion, finely chopped

3 garlic cloves, finely chopped

450g GF spaghetti or rice noodles

½ fresh red chilli, finely sliced

2 tablespoons salted capers, rinsed and chopped

2 large ripe vine tomatoes, roughly chopped

6–8 anchovies in oil, roughly chopped

4 tablespoons chopped parsley

There are some pretty good gluten-free pastas on the market now. Alternatively, use rice or soba noodles.

Serves 4 • **PREP TIME** *15 minutes* • **COOKING TIME** *20 minutes*

1. Heat the oil in a pan over a medium heat and cook the onion and garlic for about 10 minutes until softened.

2. Meanwhile, cook the spaghetti to al dente in plenty of salted boiling water, drain well and add a touch of olive oil to stop it sticking together.

3. Add the chilli and capers to the onion and garlic, and cook for a further 5 minutes. Take off the heat and add the tomatoes and anchovies. Mix well, then add the cooked pasta or rice noodles and fold through.

4. Serve in deep bowls with lots of chopped parsley.

salmon & prawn burgers

250g fresh salmon, skinned, boned and thoroughly chilled

250g freshwater prawns, chilled

1 level tablespoon grated fresh ginger

1 tablespoon GF tamari sauce

2 teaspoons sesame oil

2 tablespoons toasted sesame seeds

2 tablespoons chopped fresh Thai basil

salt and ground black pepper

3–4 GF tablespoons fresh breadcrumbs (optional)

2 tablespoons olive oil

4 medium GF burger buns

1 ripe avocado, cut into thin, long slivers

1 Little Gem lettuce, very finely shredded

2 tablespoons roughly chopped fresh tarragon

FOR THE SAUCE

4 tablespoons GF mayonnaise

2 tablespoons GF tomato ketchup

1 tablespoon Worcestershire sauce

1 tablespoon brandy

a dash of GF Tabasco sauce

4 tablespoons chopped fresh parsley

½ teaspoon smoked paprika

a pinch of cayenne pepper

For this recipe to work, the fish has to be as fresh as possible and really well chilled. I add a little whisked egg white to the mixture to help bind the fish together, but you can omit it if you prefer.

Makes 4 burgers • **PREP TIME** *15 minutes* • **COOKING TIME** *6–8 minutes*

1. Chop the salmon and prawns very finely, then refrigerate again so that they're really cold.

2. In a bowl, mix together the ginger, soy sauce, sesame oil and seeds and Thai basil, and season well with salt and pepper.

3. Scatter a few breadcrumbs, if using, over the salmon and mix together really well. Mould into four even patties, flatten and refrigerate.

4. Meanwhile, place all the ingredients for the sauce into a bowl and mix well.

5. Heat the olive oil in a large non-stick frying pan for a couple of minutes over a medium heat. Add the fish burgers and gently cook for 2–3 minutes so they take a little colour. Flip over and cook for a further 2–3 minutes, leaving the centre slightly undercooked.

6. Open up the buns and place on a board. Spread with a little of the sauce. Top with a few slivers of avocado, a little shredded lettuce and a sprinkling of tarragon.

7. Place the burgers on top, add more sauce and serve.

barbecued whole fish with avocado & banana

The Brazilians love avocado, but they eat it with sugar and other sweet accompaniments. When we were filming in Brazil, we had an avocado smoothie for breakfast, made by our security man, that was sweetened with sugar, and it was really quite good. With that in mind, here is a dish I created using local fresh fish we caught with the fisherman, stuffed with banana, garlic and honey avocado.

2 large ripe avocados
4 tablespoons clear honey
1 medium ripe banana, cut into
   1cm slices
salt and ground black pepper
3 garlic cloves, finely chopped
4 tablespoons chopped parsley
juice of 3 large limes
1kg whole fish such as bass,
   bream or John Dory, scaled,
   gutted and fins removed
olive oil
2 sprigs of coriander
2 sprigs of rosemary
2–3 spring onions
4 slices of fresh lime or lemon

Serves 4 · **PREP TIME** *25 minutes* · **COOKING TIME** *12–15 minutes*

1. Preheat the barbecue or heat a griddle.

2. Cut the avocados in half and remove the stones. Cut a small sliver off the bottom of each half so that they sit nice and securely. Score the flesh widthways and lengthways, but don't cut all the way to the skin.

3. Heat the honey in a pan over a low heat, being careful not to burn it, and sauté the banana in the honey with a little salt until nicely coloured and slightly soft. Add the garlic, parsley, salt and pepper and lime juice, then take off the heat.

4. Brush both the fish and the bars of the barbecue or the griddle with oil, then sprinkle with salt and pepper. Stuff the fish with the coriander, rosemary and spring onions and cook it for 5–6 minutes on each side. Take off the heat and let cool slightly, then flake the flesh into a bowl.

5. Fill the halved avocados with the banana mixture and top with large flakes of the barbecued fish. Sprinkle with salt, pepper and a little olive oil, and serve with the lime or lemon slices.

TIP *The golden rule when barbecuing the fish is to make sure the bars and fish are well oiled and then sprinkled with a little salt and pepper. This stops the fish sticking to the bars.*

easy mackerel teriyaki

Make sure the fish is as fresh as possible and slightly undercook it, then leave it to rest and cook through. The sauce (which will keep for a couple of months in the fridge) is used as a seasoning that coats the fish and helps it brown nicely.

4 large mackerel fillets
salt and ground black pepper
2 tablespoons olive oil

FOR THE SAUCE
150ml mirin
100ml GF tamari sauce
50ml sake (optional)
4 tablespoons caster or
   granulated sugar
1 tablespoon GF brown miso
   paste (optional)
1 tablespoon olive oil
steamed or boiled rice, to serve

Serves 4 · **PREP TIME** *10 minutes* · **COOKING TIME** *5–8 minutes*

1. Place all the ingredients for the sauce in a small pan over a low heat and simmer gently until reduced by half. The sauce should be slightly syrupy but not too thick.

2. Lay the fillets skin-side up. Make three or four long slashes just through the skin, then make four more slashes at the opposite angle so that you have a criss-cross effect. Season with salt and pepper, then spoon a couple of teaspoons of the sauce over the skin.

3. Heat a large non-stick frying pan and add the oil. Place the fish, skin-side down, into the hot oil and cook for 2–3 minutes. Spoon a couple of teaspoons of sauce over the skinless side, then flip over and cook for a further 1–2 minutes. Do not overcook the fish.

4. Lift the fish out of the pan and leave to rest on a warm plate for 5 minutes, loosely covered with foil.

5. Serve warm with the extra sauce and some steamed or boiled rice.

haddock with home-made lighter tartar sauce & twice-baked potatoes

4 x 175g haddock fillets,
    skinned and boned
2 teaspoons GF Dijon mustard
2 tablespoons GF rice flour
1 medium egg
150g GF breadcrumbs, or
    crushed GF rice cakes
2 tablespoons finely chopped
    parsley
4 tablespoons olive oil
salt and ground black pepper

FOR THE POTATOES
4 large baking potatoes, washed
2 tablespoons olive oil
2 medium onions, finely
    chopped
2 garlic cloves, chopped
4 tablespoons chopped basil
½ teaspoon paprika
salt and ground black pepper
100g Cheddar cheese, grated

FOR THE SAUCE
2 spring onions, chopped
4 heaped tablespoons low-fat
    GF mayonnaise
4 heaped tablespoons low-fat
    thick yogurt
2 tablespoons chopped
    gherkins
2 tablespoons chopped fresh
    parsley
1 tablespoon chopped capers
2 teaspoons white wine vinegar
1 teaspoon GF Dijon mustard
a pinch of sugar

This is a lighter version of fish with potatoes, but nevertheless really tasty. I use salt and vinegar rice cakes to give some extra crunch to the twice-baked potatoes. You can, of course, dip the fillets in flour, egg and breadcrumbs and deep-fry, just make sure you use gluten free flour, a clean fryer, clean oil, and make sure you dry them thoroughly first on kitchen paper.

Serves 4 · **PREP TIME** *30 minutes in total* · **COOKING TIME** *about 1½ hours*

1. First make the potatoes. Preheat the oven to 220°C/200°C fan/gas mark 7.

2. Bake the potatoes for 1 hour, or until soft and the skins are crispy.

3. Meanwhile, heat the oil in a pan over a low heat and cook the onions and garlic for 2–3 minutes until softened. Add the basil and sprinkle with paprika.

4. Remove the potatoes from the oven and cut them in half lengthways, spoon the hot flesh into a bowl, keeping the skins intact.

5. Add the onions and garlic to the bowl with a little salt and pepper, and mix carefully; do not purée. Spoon the mixture back into the potato skins, piling them nice and high. Sprinkle over the cheese and return to the oven or a hot grill for 2–3 minutes until lightly browned.

6. Meanwhile, place all the ingredients for the sauce into a bowl and mix well.

7. Now prepare the fish. Combine the breadcrumbs and parsley in a small bowl. Spoon a very thin layer of mustard over one side of the haddock fillets. Dust well in the rice flour, then brush with beaten egg. Sprinkle over the breadcrumb mixture and pat down. Turn over the fillets and repeat on the other side.

8. Heat the oil in a frying pan over a medium heat. Place the fillets in the hot oil and cook for 3–4 minutes, then flip over and cook for a further 3–4 minutes, then turn off the heat and leave to cook through for a further 2–3 minutes.

9. Serve the fish with the potatoes and sauce on the side.

spicy popcorn hake with green herb mayo

Hake is one of my favourite fish, delicate in flavour with a lovely meaty bite. This recipe makes a simple lunch or starter. Fine-grade polenta makes a lovely crunchy alternative to breadcrumbs. I really like the cornmeal coating, which tastes similar to popcorn.

vegetable oil, for deep-
frying (see note about
contamination on page 8)
2 medium eggs, lightly beaten
½ teaspoon ground cumin
a pinch of GF dried chilli
powder
400g hake, boned and cut
into 2cm strips
4 tablespoons cornflour
200g fine-ground polenta
or cornmeal

FOR THE SAUCE
350ml GF mayonnaise
2 teaspoons roughly chopped
fresh chilli
2 teaspoons GF Dijon mustard
2 large spring onions, roughly
chopped
4 tablespoons fresh green
herbs such as basil,
coriander or parsley
a small handful of fresh
spinach leaves
2 tablespoons white wine
vinegar
ground black pepper

Serves 4 • **PREP TIME** *20 minutes* • **COOKING TIME** *15–18 minutes*

1. Heat the oil to 175°C in a deep-fat fryer or deep-sided pan filled one-third with oil.

2. For the sauce, put the mayonnaise, chilli, mustard, spring onions, herbs and spinach into a liquidiser and blitz with the vinegar and a little cold water until you have a thick, green sauce. Spoon into a bowl and season with pepper.

3. In a bowl, mix the beaten eggs with the cumin and chilli.

4. Dust the hake strips in the cornflour, then coat in the egg mixture and finally the polenta or cornmeal. Fry in the oil in small batches for 3–4 minutes until crisp, turning occasionally.

5. Drain well on kitchen paper and serve with the sauce.

pan-fried loch trout with a lemon & cucumber salsa

2 tablespoons vegetable oil

1 tablespoon unsalted butter

1 tablespoon paprika

1 teaspoon salt

½ teaspoon ground black pepper

1 teaspoon dried garlic powder

4 x 150–180g fresh loch trout fillets, skinned and boned

FOR THE SALSA

½ small cucumber, finely chopped

3 spring onions, finely chopped

finely grated zest and juice of 1 large lemon

2–3 tablespoons extra virgin olive oil

2 tablespoons chopped coriander

1 tablespoon chopped fresh basil

1 tablespoon chopped fresh mint

½ teaspoon chopped fresh red chilli (optional)

a pinch of salt

a pinch of sugar

I use a lot of trout and always have, but it gets a bit of a bum deal. It's not seen as trendy, but that finally might be changing. I like its close, dense texture and colour. This dish would also work well with salmon.

Serves 4 • **PREP TIME** *10 minutes* • **COOKING TIME** *10–12 minutes*

1. Mix all the ingredients for the salsa and leave to marinate for 15 minutes.

2. Heat the oil and butter in a pan over a high heat.

3. In a small bowl, mix together the paprika, salt, pepper and garlic, then dust the fillets all over with the mixture.

4. Place the fillets into the hot oil and butter and cook for 2–3 minutes, then flip over, and cook for a further 1–2 minutes. Remove the fillets from the pan while they are still slightly undercooked and leave to rest and cook through for a few minutes. Serve warm with the salsa on the side.

baked salmon with crispy seaweed

The cooking of the salmon really is the key to this dish. The flesh needs to be really soft and succulent, so cook it halfway, then leave it for a few minutes for the residual heat to warm the fish through. The seaweed topping is a different and tasty way to season it.

4 tablespoons olive oil
4 x 200g salmon fillets, skin on
salt and ground black pepper

FOR THE TOPPING
10g GF green nori seaweed
    flakes
3 teaspoons caster sugar
¼ teaspoon ground black
    pepper
½ teaspoon garlic powder
½ teaspoon salt

FOR THE DIPPING SAUCE
6 tablespoons rice wine
    vinegar
4 tablespoons GF tamari sauce
2 teaspoons caster sugar
1 teaspoon sesame oil

Serves 4 · **PREP TIME** *5 minutes* · **COOKING TIME** *15 minutes*

1. Preheat the oven to 200°C/190°C/gas mark 6, or the grill to its highest setting.

2. Heat the oil in an ovenproof pan over a high heat.

3. Season the salmon all over with salt and pepper, and place it skin-side down into the pan. Once it's sizzling, transfer the pan to the oven or grill and cook for 4–5 minutes, then check that the fish is not overcooking. You need to take the fish out when it's cooked halfway. Remove from the oven and leave on top of the stove for 10 minutes, loosely covered with foil.

4. Meanwhile, scatter the seaweed onto an oven tray and pop it into the oven or under the grill to slightly toast. This will take less than 1 minute, so be careful not to burn it. Remove and transfer to a plate to cool.

5. Add the sugar, pepper, garlic powder and salt to the seaweed, and mix well.

6. In a small bowl, mix together all the ingredients for the sauce.

7. After 10 minutes resting, the salmon should be soft and warmed through, but not overcooked. If you gently pinch the salmon, the flakes should just come apart but still look undercooked.

8. Place the salmon fillets into four small bowls and pile over the seaweed topping.

9. Serve straight away with the dipping sauce on the side.

meat & poultry

pancetta, bean & pea pasta broth

4 tablespoon olive oil

150g pancetta or bacon, cut
　　into 5mm pieces

1 small onion, finely chopped

200g GF penne

750ml hot GF vegetable stock

200g frozen peas

200g tin cannellini, butter
　　or haricot beans, drained

ground black pepper

extra virgin olive oil, for
　　dressing

Dried beans are very good if you have the time to soak them overnight, but tinned beans are a pretty good substitute.

Serves 4 · **PREP TIME** *25 minutes* · **COOKING TIME** *20 minutes*

1. Heat 1 tablespoon of oil in a pan over a medium heat and cook the pancetta until well browned. Add the onion, cook for 1 minute, then add the pasta and stock. Bring to the boil, reduce the heat and simmer for 10 minutes until the pasta is just cooked.

2. Add the peas and beans to the pan, and bring back to the boil, then immediately take off the heat. Drain well and toss in 2–3 tablespoons of olive oil.

3. Check the seasoning and dress with a little extra virgin oil to finish, then serve.

flageolet & chicken liver broth with olive oil

6 tablespoons olive oil

2 small onions, diced

2 large carrots, chopped

2 celery sticks, chopped

2 whole garlic cloves, peeled

400g tin flageolet beans,
　　rinsed

2 bay leaves

2 x 10g GF chicken stock cubes

salt and ground black pepper

225g fresh chicken livers,
　　trimmed

a pinch of caster sugar

This sounds an unlikely combination, but it works. The secret is not to use too many livers and not to leave out the olive oil – it's an essential component. It makes a great main course or starter.

Serves 4 · **PREP TIME** *25 minutes* · **COOKING TIME** *30–40 minutes*

1. Heat 2 tablespoons of the oil in a pan over a low heat and cook the onions, carrots, celery and garlic for 10 minutes until softened.

2. Add 300g of the beans, the bay leaves, 1.5 litres of hot water and the stock cubes, season well and bring to the boil. Reduce the heat and simmer for about 20 minutes.

3. When the carrots are cooked, add the livers and simmer for a few minutes, then transfer to a blender and blend until smooth. You may need to add a touch more stock if the broth is too thick. Return to the pan to heat through, check the seasoning and add the sugar.

4. To serve, pop a few of the remaining beans in the bottom of serving bowls and pour over the broth. Spoon over the remaining olive oil and a good grinding of pepper.

Penang fried chicken with cashew nuts, garlic & chilli

I cooked this dish in a market in Penang, Malaysia, during a 20-minute break from a rail trip on the Eastern Oriental Express. It's so simple, but really effective, and only took a few minutes to film. The locals loved seeing an English boy trying to cook the local cuisine.

3 tablespoons vegetable oil

350g chopped chicken thigh meat, skin on

1 small onion, very finely chopped

2 garlic cloves, crushed

1–2 tablespoons GF Penang red curry paste

2 lemongrass stems, cut in half and bruised

2 teaspoons Thai shrimp paste

150ml GF coconut milk

4–6 tablespoons tamarind pulp or juice

salt and ground black pepper

4 tablespoons chopped unsalted cashew nuts, to garnish

2 medium chillies, finely chopped, to garnish

a pinch of sugar

Serves 4 · **PREP TIME** *20 minutes* · **COOKING TIME** *10 minutes*

1. Heat 2 tablespoons of the oil in a wok or frying pan over a high heat. Cook the chicken until sealed and well coloured but only half cooked. Transfer to a bowl and keep warm.

2. Add the remaining oil to the pan and cook the onion, garlic and red curry paste for 2–3 minutes. Add the lemongrass and shrimp paste, breaking it up with a spoon, then the coconut milk and tamarind, and bring to the boil.

3. Tip the chicken back into the pan and finish cooking it in the sauce, but do not overcook it.

4. Season well with salt and pepper and serve in deep bowls, sprinkled with the cashew nuts, the chillies and a small sprinkling of sugar.

chicken, leek & chorizo pie

This is a nice, easy pie to prepare and cook. If you can make and chill the mix first, all the better. Make sure the mix isn't over-thickened or the pie will be difficult to eat. If you don't have any chorizo, cooked ham works just as well.

1 medium onion, finely diced
2 garlic cloves, chopped
2 medium leeks, finely
   chopped
12 medium chicken thighs,
   bone in
2 x 10g GF chicken stock cubes
4 tablespoons cornflour,
   arrowroot or other starch
150g frozen peas
150g cooking chorizo or
   cooked ham, cubed
200g tin sweetcorn, drained
salt and ground black pepper
1 quantity GF Shortcrust Pastry
   (page 41)
1 egg, beaten

Serves 4–6 · **PREP TIME** *20 minutes* · **COOKING TIME** *50 minutes*

1. Preheat the oven to 200°C/190°C fan/gas mark 6.

2. Place the onion, garlic, leeks, chicken and stock cubes into a pan over a high heat. Just cover with cold water and bring to the boil. Reduce the heat and simmer for 20 minutes, or until the chicken is cooked but not falling off the bone.

3. Lift the chicken thighs out of the pan and bring the stock back to the boil. Cook for 5 minutes to thicken.

4. Meanwhile remove the skin from the chicken and discard, then pull the meat away from the bone. Roughly chop, then return the chicken to the pan of reduced stock. Take off the heat and mix well. There should be enough sauce to cover the meat well, but the mixture shouldn't be too sloppy. Return to a simmer.

5. Mix the cornflour with 4 tablespoons of cold water and gently pour into the pan. The stock will thicken almost straight away.

6. Add the peas, chorizo or ham and sweetcorn, and season with salt and pepper. The mix should be nice and thick now.

7. Spoon the mixture into a 26 x 19cm deep rectangular dish. Cool and chill.

8. Roll out the dough to roughly the size and shape of your pie dish. Trim the edges and set the trimmings aside (don't roll them up).

9. Brush the rim of the baking dish with the beaten egg and lay the pastry trimmings around the edge to cover it. Press the trimmings gently, then brush them with egg. Carefully lay the pastry lid over the dish, pressing it down well into the trimmings to seal. Decorate the edges by pinching with your fingers or pressing down with the prongs of a fork. Brush all over with beaten egg, then make two or three slits in the top of the pie to let out any steam while cooking.

10. Bake for 35–40 minutes, cool for 10 minutes, then serve.

crispy fried chilli chicken

The combination of flavours here is so satisfying. I sometimes prepare turkey, pork and even pheasant this way. Just remember to deep-fry in small batches to get a crisp finish.

vegetable oil, for deep-frying (see note about contamination on page 8)

½ small red pepper, very thinly sliced

5 spring onions, very finely sliced

3 garlic cloves, finely chopped

2 tablespoons GF tamari sauce

4 tablespoons GF sweet chilli sauce

3 tablespoons GF tomato ketchup

5 tablespoons white wine vinegar or cider vinegar

white of ½ medium egg

2–3 heaped tablespoons cornflour

1 tablespoon sesame seeds (optional)

300g chicken breast (about 2 medium), skinned and cut into very thin strips

200g cooked GF rice noodles, to serve

1 tablespoon finely chopped fresh red chilli, to garnish

Serves 4 · **PREP TIME** *25 minutes* · **COOKING TIME** *25 minutes*

1. Fill a wok or deep frying pan to just under halfway with oil and heat to about 190°C.

2. Heat a separate pan over a high heat. Transfer about 2 tablespoons of hot oil from the wok into the pan, then add the red pepper, spring onions and garlic, and sauté quickly for 2–3 minutes. Add the tamari, chilli sauce, ketchup and vinegar, mix well and bring to the boil. Simmer for 2–3 minutes until the sauce has thickened somewhat.

3. In a bowl, whisk together the egg white, cornflour and sesame seeds, if using. The mixture should have the texture and look of thick cream. Add the chicken and coat really well.

4. Gently fry the strips of chicken in the hot oil for 2–3 minutes, turning occasionally. You may have to do this in three or four batches so the heat stays in the oil.

5. Just before serving, coat the crispy chicken in the sauce. Serve straight away on top of rice noodles and sprinkle with a little finely sliced fresh red chilli.

chicken & egg-fried noodles

1 small carrot, cut into batons

1 red pepper, finely sliced

salt

200g GF fine glass rice noodles

2 tablespoons vegetable oil

1 tablespoon chopped fresh
   ginger

½ red jalapeño chilli, finely
   chopped

½ teaspoon ground turmeric

1 medium egg, beaten

about 200g leftover cooked
   chicken, turkey or pork

225g tin water chestnuts,
   drained and chopped

100g beansprouts

2 tablespoons rice vinegar

2 tablespoons GF tamari sauce

Any cooked light meat, such as pork or turkey, is good in this dish, or try shellfish or even tinned tuna. Just remember to stir the egg in quickly and really cook it until it's nice and dry.

Serves 4 • **PREP TIME** *20 minutes* • **COOKING TIME** *15–20 minutes*

1. Put the carrot and red pepper in a pan, cover with cold water, add a little salt, bring to the boil, then immediately lift out with a slotted spoon and transfer to a plate. Bring the water back to the boil, take the pan off the heat, add the noodles and leave for 20 minutes.

2. Heat the oil in a wok. Cook the ginger, chilli and turmeric for 2–3 minutes. Add the egg and stir vigorously until dry and broken up. Add the meat and carrot, and mix well. Add the water chestnuts, beansprouts, vinegar and tamari, and season well. Finally, add the cooked noodles, stir and serve.

easy pad Thai noodles

200g GF rice noodles

4 tablespoons olive oil

2 large garlic cloves, crushed

½ teaspoon chilli flakes

150g chicken thigh meat, finely
   shredded

350g prawns, roughly chopped

2 teaspoons nam pla fish sauce

1 tablespoon palm sugar

2 tablespoons tamarind paste

juice of 1 large lime

6 spring onions, chopped

75g beansprouts

2 tablespoons chopped
   Thai basil

2 tablespoons chopped fresh
   coriander

75g GF chopped dry-roasted
   peanuts

I sometimes omit all meat and fish and have a vegetable version with baby sweetcorn, green beans, peas and lots of baby spinach leaves. Chopped hard-boiled eggs also work really well.

Serves 4–6 • **PREP TIME** *25 minutes* • **COOKING TIME** *10 minutes*

1. Place the noodles into a large bowl and cover with boiling salted water. Leave for 10 minutes to soften and swell.

2. Meanwhile, heat the oil in a pan over a high heat and add the garlic, chilli and chicken pieces. Sauté for 2–3 minutes or until just cooked through. Add the prawns and continue to cook for 2–3 minutes.

3. Stir in the noodles, fish sauce, sugar and tamarind paste, and bring to the boil. Once reduced slightly, remove from the heat and add the lime juice, spring onions and beansprouts, and mix well. Serve in small bowls topped with the basil, coriander and a sprinkling of peanuts.

slow-cooked (pulled) turkey legs with crunchy red onion & garlic 'baconnaise'

2 medium turkey legs, or
 4 smaller ones (about 2kg)

3 tablespoons unsalted butter

2 red onions, finely chopped

2 garlic cloves, crushed

2 tablespoons fresh ginger,
 finely chopped

1 tablespoon sweet paprika

½ teaspoon GF chilli powder

1 tablespoon GF English
 mustard

4 large ripe tomatoes, chopped

4 tablespoons Worcestershire
 sauce

4 tablespoons GF tomato
 ketchup

2 tablespoons molasses sugar

2 tablespoons white wine
 vinegar

2 tablespoons tamarind
 paste

salt and ground black pepper

2 tablespoons cornflour or
 arrowroot (optional)

FOR THE 'BACONNAISE'

1 small red onion, finely
 chopped

2 garlic cloves, smoked or
 fresh, very finely chopped

8 heaped tablespoons GF
 mayonnaise

a pinch of GF hot chilli powder

2 tablespoons chopped fresh
 parsley

6 streaky bacon rashers, or
 4–6 tablespoons GF bacon
 bits

Turkey leg is rarely eaten on its own these days and I'm not sure why; I think it's delicious. The secret is to cook it very gently in a moist environment until the meat is falling off the bone, so take care not to rush it, and keep the pan tightly covered with foil or a lid at all times during the cooking. You'll end up with not only a beautifully cooked piece of moist meat, but also a wonderful sauce. In fact, I sometimes have the sauce on its own over plain steamed or boiled rice.

Serves 4 · **PREP TIME** *15 minutes* · **COOKING TIME** *about 2 hours 15 minutes*

1. Preheat the oven to 180°C/gas mark 4.

2. Nick the drumstick through the knuckle with a sharp knife. This will stop the leg springing open when it cooks and means you can use a smaller pan.

3. Put a large casserole or heavy pan on a medium heat and melt the butter. Add the onions and garlic, and cook for 10 minutes. Add the ginger, paprika and chilli powder, and cook for a further 5 minutes, then add the mustard, tomatoes, Worcestershire sauce, ketchup, molasses sugar, vinegar and tamarind along with a glass of cold water. Season well with salt and pepper and bring to the boil.

4. Add the turkey leg and coat in the sauce, then put the lid on the pot and pop it in the oven. Cook for 1 hour, then turn the drumstick over and cook for a further 1 hour, or until the meat is perfectly cooked (see below).

5. Meanwhile, make the 'baconnaise' by combining all the ingredients in a small bowl.

6. Carefully remove the cooked drumstick from the pan and keep warm. Transfer all the cooking liquid to a food-processor and blitz until you have a smooth sauce. You can thicken it slightly with the cornflour slaked in a little cold water, but don't go mad. Adjust the seasoning with salt, pepper, sugar and vinegar.

7. Serve the turkey meat with mash or crisp chips and the 'baconnaise' on the side.

TIP *Turkey legs vary greatly, so judge whether it's cooked by eye and by touch. The meat should fall off the bone when prised away with two forks, but not be dry and overcooked; if the meat is dry, then the oven was too hot and the meat cooked too quickly.*

spicy crisp sesame turkey with garlic & parsley mayo

It's fun to serve this very tasty turkey in small silicone paper cones. Make sure you coat the turkey really well in the flour and fry it in small batches to keep the oil hot.

450g turkey breast, thinly cut
1 tablespoon nam pla fish
   sauce
2 pinches of ground black
   pepper
a pinch of dried chilli
1 tablespoon sesame seeds
200g tapioca flour or
   arrowroot
vegetable oil, for deep-
   frying (see note about
   contamination on page 8)
salt

FOR THE MAYONNAISE
6 tablespoons GF mayonnaise
2 garlic cloves, crushed
4 tablespoons chopped
   flat-leaf parsley

Serves 4 • **PREP TIME** *15 minutes* • **COOKING TIME** *10 minutes*

1. Mix together all the ingredients for the mayonnaise.

2. Lay the turkey breast on a large piece of cling film and wet with a little water (this will help the meat to spread thinner when pressed). Cover with a second piece of cling film. Using a rolling pin, gently flatten the turkey to 2mm thick and you can almost see through the meat. Carefully lift the cling film off and transfer the meat to a chopping board; don't worry if it tears. Finely slice or shred the meat.

3. In a bowl, mix together the fish sauce, pepper, chilli and sesame seeds. Add the turkey and coat well.

4. Put the tapioca flour in a bowl. Tip the spiced meat into it and coat really well, then place the meat into a small sieve and dust off the excess flour.

5. Heat the vegetable oil to 185°C in a deep-fryer or deep-sided pan filled one-third with oil.

6. Fry the turkey in small batches for 1–2 minutes, then drain on kitchen paper and sprinkle with a little salt. Serve hot with the mayonnaise on the side.

chorizo & smoked chicken empanadas

This is a lovely smokey combination. Do not over fill or they will split.

1 quantity Empanada Dough
 (opposite)
4 tablespoons extra virgin
 olive oil
1 small onion, finely chopped
2 garlic cloves, finely chopped
150g cooking chorizo,
 very finely chopped
150g smoked chicken,
 very finely chopped
salt and ground black pepper
vegetable oil, for deep-
 frying (see note about
 contamination on page 8)

Serves 4 • **PREP TIME** *15 minutes* • **COOKING TIME** *12–15 minutes in batches*

1. Heat the olive oil in a pan over a low heat and cook the onion and garlic for about 10 minutes to soften really well. Remove from the heat and spoon into a bowl with the chorizo and chicken. Mix well and season with salt and pepper .

2. Heat the vegetable oil to 180°C in a deep-sided pan filled one-third with oil.

3. Roll out the dough with a dusting of gluten-free flour. Use a 6cm cutter to cut out circles, then brush the edges with a little beaten egg. Fill one side, then fold over the dough and press well. Press the edge with a fork to get a nicer seal and appearance.

4. Deep-fry for 2–3 minutes until blistered and cooked through, turning occasionally to colour evenly.

my quick feijoada

2 x 400g tins butter or
 cannellini beans, drained
2 x 10g GF pork
 stock cubes
3 tablespoons vegetable oil
3 small onions, chopped
400g cooked andouille or any
 GF cured cooked smoked
 sausage, chopped
400g cooked smoked ham,
 cubed
8 garlic cloves, crushed
juice of 1 large orange
200g white cabbage, chard,
 cavolo nero or spinach,
 very finely shredded
salt and ground black pepper
boiled rice, to serve

A twist on the traditional Portuguese beef, pork and bean stew that's also a popular dish in Brazil. I use white beans instead of black, plus I use cooked ham, which makes cooking a lot quicker.

Serves 4 • **PREP TIME** *20 minutes* • **COOKING TIME** *45–50 minutes*

1. Put the beans in a pan over a medium heat and cover with cold water. Add the stock cubes and bring to a simmer.

2. Meanwhile heat the oil in a frying pan over a low heat and fry the onions for about 10 minutes until soft.

3. Add the sausage and ham to the beans with the cooked onions, garlic and orange juice. Leave to simmer gently for about 45 minutes, topping up with water as necessary, then add the cabbage or spinach and cook for a further 5 minutes.

4. Season to taste and serve with boiled rice.

empanada dough

This recipe is very simple but makes fabulous deep-fried morsels. The mix also freezes well once the empanadas are finished. Then when you want to serve them, cook straight from the freezer. The only word of caution: cut the margarine into small cubes (or melt it first) as prolonged simmering reduces the water by evaporation, which can change the structure of the recipe. The same can be said for choux pastry.

300g GF plain flour
(I sometimes use the GF
White Bread Flour Blend,
page 15, as this makes
a crisper end result)
¼ teaspoon salt
120g hard baking margarine,
cut into small cubes

Makes enough for 20 small empanadas • **PREP TIME** *10 minutes*
• **COOKING TIME** *10 minutes*

1. Place the flour and salt into a mixing bowl.

2. Place the margarine and 250ml of cold water into a saucepan and bring to a simmer stirring well.

3. Once melted, immediately add the flour to the water and margarine (see tip below). Beat well, off the heat, until the dough no longer sticks to the sides of the pan, then beat for a further 2 minutes.

4. Turn out onto a board lightly dusted with gluten-free flour and bring the dough together.

5. Flatten and roll between two sheets of cling film and then chill until the dough is cold and firm.

6. When nicely chilled, cut, knead again and use.

TIP *To add the flour to the water and margarine mixture as quickly as possible, fold a piece of greaseproof paper in half and use it to 'shoot' the flour into the pan in one go.*

turkey enchiladas

This dish can be made with either gluten-free tortilla wraps, or pliable corn tortillas. The recipe for tortillas on page 34 works very well. Your enchiladas should not be swimming in sauce but well coated with a firm mixture that's easy to roll, and it's important to melt the cheese to make this dish really delicious.

2 tablespoons vegetable oil,
   plus extra for greasing
2 small onions, diced
2 garlic cloves, chopped
400g tin chopped tomatoes
1 x 10g GF vegetable stock
   cube
¼ teaspoon GF chilli powder
1 teaspoon dried oregano
350g turkey mince
salt
8 small pliable GF corn tortillas
200g Cheddar cheese, grated
150ml soured cream, to serve

Serves 4 · **PREP TIME** *20 minutes* · **COOKING TIME** *30 minutes*

1. Preheat the oven to 200°C/gas mark 6, or the grill to its highest setting. Grease a baking dish with a little oil.

2. Heat the oil in a medium pan over a low heat and cook the onions and garlic for 10 minutes. Add the tomatoes, 200ml of cold water, the stock cube, chilli, oregano and mince to the pan. Mix really well then simmer for 15 minutes. Once thickened, season well with salt. Set half the turkey mixture aside.

3. Place a little of the turkey into a tortilla. Add a little cheese, roll up and place in the prepared baking dish, then repeat until you've filled all eight tortillas. The tighter you can pack them in the dish, the better.

4. Spoon over the rest of the mince and the remaining cheese. Bake for 15 minutes to brown, or quickly brown under the grill. Serve with soured cream.

moussaka

Years ago I spent a few months in Greece. It was great fun, but on the whole the food was pretty uninspiring – the coffee was the sweetest I have ever drunk! However, I have fond memories of a few special dishes, such as wonderful deep-fried whole squid, butter beans braised in a rich, dense gravy, and moussaka, made by the lady of the house (she also made incredible lamb and goat dishes). This is based on her recipe, and I usually serve it with tzatziki.

---

2 medium potatoes, skin on
6 tablespoons olive oil
1 aubergine, cut lengthways
    into 1cm slices
salt and ground black pepper
2 onions, diced
2 teaspoons dried oregano
2 garlic cloves, crushed
500g lamb mince
1 x 10g GF lamb
    or beef stock cube
6 tablespoons tomato purée
300ml warm milk
30g butter, very soft
25g cornflour
4 ripe tomatoes, blanched,
    peeled and sliced

Serves 4 · **PREP TIME** *40 minutes* · **COOKING TIME** *40 minutes*

1. Preheat the oven to 200°C/190°C fan/gas mark 6.

2. Boil the potatoes in a pan of water over a high heat until tender and a knife passes through them easily. Remove from the pan and leave to cool, then peel and slice into 1cm thick slices.

3. Heat half the oil in a pan, add the aubergine slices and season well with salt and pepper, then cook on both sides until browned. Remove from the pan and drain on kitchen paper.

4. Add the remaining oil to the pan with the onions, oregano and garlic, and cook over a low heat for 2–3 minutes until softened. Add the mince and stock cube, and brown the meat. Add 300–400ml of cold water to the mince along with the tomato purée, then cook for 15–20 minutes until you have a thick stew consistency.

5. Meanwhile, pour the milk into a pan over a medium heat and bring to a simmer. In a small bowl, mix together the butter and cornflour, then add to the milk; the mixture will thicken almost straight away. Remove the pan from the heat and season well with salt and pepper.

6. To assemble the moussaka, spoon half the mince into the bottom of a 20 x 25 x 5cm-deep baking dish and top with the tomato slices. Add the rest of the mince in a layer then top with the aubergines. Press down well, then add the potatoes and press down well again. Finally, pour over the sauce. Bake for 20–25 minutes or until well browned and heated through. Leave to rest for 15 minutes to cool slightly before serving.

succulent lamb shanks with chickpeas & chorizo

2 tablespoons olive oil

1 onion, diced

3 garlic cloves, crushed

5 sprigs of rosemary

2 teaspoons chopped red chilli

2 large (about 200g) cooking
   chorizo sausages, cut into
   4 pieces

400g tin chickpeas, drained

1 x 10g GF chicken stock cube

300ml boiling water

3 tablespoons white wine
   vinegar

salt and ground black pepper

2 small lamb shanks

mashed potatoes and mint
   sauce, to serve

This simple stew can be made in advance and left for a day or so in the fridge, or it can be cooked and frozen for a later date. The lamb, combined with the chorizo and chickpeas, makes a lovely flavour, texture and colour combination.

Serves 2 · **PREP TIME** *15 minutes* · **COOKING TIME** *about 1 hour 45 minutes*

1. Preheat the oven to 180°C/160°C fan/gas mark 4.

2. Heat the oil in a heavy-based saucepan and cook the onion, garlic, rosemary and chilli for a couple of minutes. Add the chorizo pieces and stir well.

3. Add the chickpeas, stock cube, boiling water, vinegar and season with salt and pepper. Stir well, then place the lamb shanks on top, coating them with the water. Bring to the boil, cover and transfer to the oven.

4. Cook for 1 hour 45 minutes, by which time the meat will be very tender but not falling off the bone. Skim off a little of the fat.

5. Serve in deep bowls with mashed potatoes and mint sauce.

my lamb tagine

2 heaped teaspoons crushed
black peppercorns
2 heaped teaspoons crushed
whole coriander seeds
2 heaped teaspoons ground
cinnamon
1 heaped teaspoon freshly
grated nutmeg
750g boned shoulder of lamb,
cut into 3–4cm pieces
1 litre hot strong GF chicken
or lamb stock
4 tablespoons vegetable oil
4 medium onions, finely sliced
4 garlic cloves, roughly
chopped
4 tablespoons GF Flour Mix
A (page 15)
3 tablespoons tomato purée
500ml fresh orange juice
juice and finely grated zest
of 1 large lemon
140g 'ready-to-eat' dried
prunes, stoned and roughly
chopped
115g dried apricots, roughly
chopped
85g raisins
a pinch of sugar
salt

Years ago I filmed a show in Tunisia and the last meal we cooked was this dish. It went down a storm and for years afterwards I cooked it in my restaurant, even making a pie out of it. It does take a little time but it is well worth the effort. I have found that, left in the fridge for a couple of days, the flavours improve even more.

Serves 6–8 · **PREP TIME** *20 minutes* · **COOKING TIME** *about 1½ hours*

1. Preheat the oven to 160°C/150°C fan/gas mark 3.

2. Mix all the spices together in a large bowl. Add the meat and coat well in the spices.

3. Put the stock in a pan over a high heat and bring to the boil.

4. Heat 3 tablespoons of the oil in a frying pan over a medium heat and cook the lamb in small batches until lightly browned. Do not burn the spices. Transfer the meat to a colander to drain well.

5. Add the remaining oil to the pan and cook the onions and garlic for 5–10 minutes to soften slightly.

6. Place the meat in a deep pan or casserole. Add the gluten-free flour and tomato purée, and stir well, then add the fried onions and mix again. Add the orange juice and enough of the boiling hot stock to just cover the meat. Remember, the lamb will release quite a lot of moisture. Add the lemon juice and zest and the dried fruits, and mix well. Finally, add the sugar and salt, to taste.

7. Bring to a simmer over a medium heat, stirring all the time, cover with a tight-fitting lid and transfer to the oven to cook for 1½ hours, or until the meat is soft and tender but not overcooked.

8. Serve with steamed rice.

slow-roast shoulder of lamb with Bramley apple & mint glaze

3–4 tablespoons vegetable oil

2 sweet potatoes, peeled and cut into long wedges

2 red onions, cut into large wedges

1 small butternut squash, deseeded and cut into long wedges

1 red pepper, deseeded and chopped into large chunks

1 green pepper, deseeded and chopped into large chunks

1 yellow pepper, deseeded and chopped into large chunks

1 small head of celery, cut lengthways into 6–8 stalks

1 shoulder of British lamb (about 1.5kg)

salt and ground black pepper

FOR THE GLAZE

1 large Bramley apple, peeled, cored and roughly chopped

2 tablespoons white wine vinegar

1 small jar mint jelly (about 200g)

a small bunch of fresh mint, chopped

ground black pepper

FOR THE GRAVY

500ml hot strong GF lamb stock

salt and ground black pepper

2 tablespoons cornfour or arrowroot

I find that joints from the front of the animal tend to make good roasts. This is because they're slightly fattier than those from the rear. The fat also means that you can slow-roast for longer and almost overcook a fore joint and it will still taste great, whereas the leg, for instance, can dry out considerably during long cooking. The glaze is a simple one, but finishes the dish really well. Any roasted vegetables will work here and the lovely flavour you gain from cooking them in the lamb juices is very tasty.

Serves 4–6 · **PREP TIME** *20–25 minutes* · **COOKING TIME** *2½ hours*

1. Preheat the oven to 190°C/180°C fan/gas mark 4. Pour the oil into a large roasting tin and place it in the oven to heat up.

2. Add all the vegetables to the hot roasting tin and turn to coat in the oil. Place the lamb on top of the vegetables and season the meat and vegetables well.

3. Roast for about 2 hours, turning the vegetables occasionally as they soak up the wonderful lamb juices. If you think they are overcooking, spoon the veg into a dish and keep warm.

4. Make the glaze by placing the apple and vinegar into a pan over a low heat. Cook gently until you have a dryish pulp, then add the mint jelly and warm through until dissolved. Add the fresh mint and season with pepper. Forty-five minutes before the lamb is ready to come out of the oven, spoon over half the glaze and return the meat to the oven to finish cooking.

5. Once cooked, remove the meat from the oven, lift it onto a large plate and cover with foil for 30 minutes, or longer if possible.

6. Meanwhile, tip any excess fat out of the roasting tin and pour the lamb juices and any lovely crispy bits of lamb and vegetables into a pan to make the gravy. Add the stock and bring to the boil, stirring. Simmer for 2–3 minutes, then check the seasoning, adjusting to taste. Thicken with a little cornflour or arrowroot.

7. Serve the lamb carved, surrounded with the vegetables and with the gravy and the rest of the glaze on the side.

glazed sausages with bean spinach & pea casserole

This tasty dish makes a great supper or light lunch. You can swap in any beans here, or add any green vegetable to suit. I sometimes serve it with mashed or baked potatoes.

70ml extra virgin olive oil
1 red onion, very finely diced
2 garlic cloves, crushed
2 tablespoons finely chopped fresh ginger
2 tablespoons tomato purée
400g tin chopped tomatoes
2 x 10g GF vegetable stock cubes
400g tin haricot beans
400g tin borlotti beans
400g tin chickpeas
150g frozen peas
100g baby spinach leaves
1 tablespoon vegetable oil
500g GF chipolatas, halved
2 teaspoons ground cumin
2 teaspoons GF garam masala
2 tablespoons GF mango chutney
1 tablespoon white wine vinegar or cider vinegar
griddled GF pitta bread and fresh coriander, to serve

Serves 4–6 · **PREP TIME** *30 minutes* · **COOKING TIME** *30 minutes*

1. Heat the olive oil in a pan and cook the onion, garlic and ginger for 10 minutes to colour up well. Add the tomato purée and tomatoes, and cook for 5 minutes. Add the stock cubes, all the beans and 200ml of cold water. Bring to the boil and simmer down to a stew for about 10 minutes. Once nice and thick, add the peas and spinach and just warm through.

2. Meanwhile, heat the oil in a frying pan over a low heat and gently fry the chipolatas until cooked and golden. Add the spices and cook for a further 3–4 minutes to release their flavours. Add the chutney and vinegar, and cook until the sausages are well coated.

3. Serve with griddled gluten-free pitta bread and fresh chopped coriander.

breakfast 'congee' rice porridge with pork

2 tablespoons vegetable oil

150g very lean pork, cut into
fine strips

500g short-grain rice

1 egg, beaten

4 tablespoons very finely
chopped spring onions

2 tablespoons chopped fresh
coriander

2 tablespoons chopped
Thai basil

4 tablespoons GF Thai hot
sauce (nam pric)

4 tablespoons chopped
roasted peanuts

juice of 2 large limes

2 tablespoons garlic oil

Congee is a thick rice broth that is served primarily for breakfast.
Almost anything can be added to give flavour and texture, though
it's always served with hot sauce, peanuts and herbs.

Serves 4 · **PREP TIME** *10 minutes* · **COOKING TIME** *20 minutes*

1. Heat the oil in a wok or large frying pan over a high heat and cook the pork for
a few seconds to almost scorch it, then remove and keep warm.

2. Cover the rice with water and gently simmer for about 15–20 minutes, or until
you have a porridge consistency. Remove from the heat and spoon into bowls.

3. Stir in a little beaten egg, which will partially cook in the hot porridge, followed by
the cooked pork, then sprinkle with the spring onions and herbs. Follow with a big
spoonful of the hot sauce and top with the peanuts. Pour over a little lime juice and
garlic oil to finish.

farfalle with ham, peas, basil & Parmesan

400g GF Rich Pasta Dough
(page 39), divided into 4

GF flour, but not pure starch,
for dusting

2 tablespoons vegetable oil

250g pancetta, smoked bacon
or cooked ham

1 medium onion, finely diced

½ vegetable or chicken GF
stock cube

250g peas

4 tablespoons chopped
fresh basil

4 tablespoons freshly grated
Parmesan cheese

salt and ground black pepper

You're aiming for a very light pea and ham stock here, the accent
being on flavour, with a few simple ingredients. Be quick and firm
when shaping the pasta bows or they will spring apart during cooking.

Serves 4 · **PREP TIME** *20 minutes* · **COOKING TIME** *20 minutes*

1. Roll out each piece of dough as thinly as possible on a surface lightly dusted with
gluten-free flour. Use a sharp knife to cut strips roughly 5 x 3cm. Quickly and firmly
pinch each piece of pasta in the middle to form a bow shape.

2. Heat the oil in a pan and sauté the pancetta until just coloured. Add the onion
and soften for 10 minutes. Add 300ml of cold water, the stock cube and peas. Bring
to the boil and cook for 1 minute. Add the basil and half the cheese to warm through.

3. Meanwhile, bring a large pan of salted water to the boil and cook the pasta for
2–3 minutes. Drain, add the pasta to the stock mixture and stir well. Spoon into deep
bowls and sprinkle over the remaining cheese.

crispy, juicy coconut pork with chilli sambal

I picked up this recipe on my travels in Sri Lanka a few years ago. I would have it for breakfast, and what a nice way it was to set up the day, though it can be eaten at other times. I've quick-brined the pork first for added succulence and flavour.

1 tablespoon salt

1 tablespoon caster sugar

4 pork chops, weighing roughly 220g each

¼ teaspoon red chilli flakes

¼ teaspoon paprika

grated zest of 1 small lime

75g fine polenta

50g desiccated coconut

2 tablespoons any starch such as tapioca, cornflour or arrowroot

1 medium egg, beaten

FOR THE SAMBAL

60g desiccated coconut

1½ tablespoons olive oil

½ small green chilli, very finely chopped

½ teaspoon black or yellow mustard seeds

3 curry leaves

salt and ground black pepper

juice of ½ lime

2 tablespoons chopped coriander

Serves 4 · **PREP TIME** *25 minutes* · **COOKING TIME** *20 minutes*

1. In a small bowl, mix together the salt and sugar.

2. Place the pork chops into a china, glass or stainless steel bowl. Spoon over half the sugar and salt mixture and rub it into the chops well. Turn them over and rub in the rest of the mixture. Leave for 10 minutes, then turn the chops over again and rub well. You will see a little liquid coming from the chops. Marinate for a further 10 minutes, then rinse under cold water and pat dry with kitchen paper.

3. Mix together the chilli, paprika and lime zest, and sprinkle over the pork chops.

4. Mix together the polenta and coconut. Dust the chops in the starch, then dip them in the beaten egg and finally the polenta and coconut mixture. Make sure both sides are coated well. Chill until needed.

5. Next, make the sambal. Place the coconut in a small bowl and pour over enough boiling water until just covered, then leave for 20 minutes to soften.

6. Meanwhile, heat the oil and gently fry the chilli, mustard seeds and curry leaves for 2 minutes.

7. Gently squeeze most of the water out of the coconut and discard. Add the fried spices to the coconut and mix well. Season with salt and pepper, then stir through the lime juice and coriander.

8. Heat a little oil and gently cook the pork chops for 4–5 minutes on each side until cooked and golden. Remove from the pan and rest on kitchen paper for 5 minutes, then serve with the sambal on the side.

easy sweet & sour meatballs with ginger & lime

The mayonnaise in these meatballs helps to keep them juicy but not fatty, while the vegetables are seasoned with tamari, honey and pepper, with no additional salt. I also like to eat them lightly chilled in a salad.

Serves 4 · **PREP TIME** *25 minutes* · **COOKING TIME** *15 minutes*

FOR THE MEATBALLS
500g pork shoulder mince
2 garlic cloves, crushed
1 small onion, very finely diced
zest and juice of 1 large lime
225g tin water chestnuts, drained and very finely chopped
1 heaped tablespoon very finely chopped fresh ginger
1 tablespoon GF tamari sauce
1 tablespoon GF mayonnaise
2 teaspoons cornflour
¼ teaspoon dried chilli flakes

FOR THE SWEET AND SOUR VEGETABLES
3 tablespoons vegetable oil
1 medium carrot, peeled and sliced into very thin strips
2 pak choi, sliced diagonally
50g baby spinach leaves
1 tablespoon clear honey
2 tablespoons GF tamari sauce
juice of 1 small lime
ground black pepper

1. In a big bowl, mix together all the ingredients for the meatballs really well. Roll into balls the size of a 50p coin, then chill really well.

2. Heat 2 tablespoons of the oil in a wok, add the meatballs and cook gently for 8–10 minutes, turning occasionally to get a nice glaze all over. Once cooked remove from the pan and keep warm.

3. Add the remaining oil to the pan. Add the carrot, pak choi and spinach, and wilt for 2–3 minutes, then add the honey, tamari and lime juice and stir through. Season with pepper.

4. Add the meatballs to the pan, stir through to heat, then serve.

pulled pork with home-made barbecue sauce

1.5kg pork shoulder, skinned and boned

200ml apple juice

6–8 buns

GF coleslaw, to serve

FOR THE RUB

1 tablespoon sweet paprika

4 teaspoons soft light brown sugar

1 teaspoon GF chilli powder

1 teaspoon celery salt

1 teaspoon garlic powder

1 teaspoon English mustard powder

1 teaspoon ground black pepper

½ teaspoon salt

FOR THE BARBECUE SAUCE

100ml olive oil

1 medium onion, finely chopped

1 red pepper, finely chopped

2 garlic cloves, chopped

175ml passata

150ml pineapple juice

125ml GF tomato ketchup

50ml cider vinegar

juice of 1 lemon

3 tablespoons light brown sugar

3 tablespoons GF Dijon mustard

2 teaspoons Tabasco sauce

1 tablespoon black treacle

1 teaspoon GF English mustard powder

1 teaspoon ground black pepper

1 teaspoon salt

Once you've put all the powerful flavours in this recipe together you end up with one of life's great dishes. I went to the heart of the North Carolina Mountains to learn how to make pulled pork. There, all the pork butts (shoulders) are rubbed and then smoked for hours on end using traditional methods. This simplified version cooks in a lot less time, but it still relies on long, slow cooking, so don't rush it. Pork belly can be substituted if you want.

Serves 6–8 • **PREP TIME** *30 minutes* • **COOKING TIME** *about 2½ hours*

1. Mix together all the ingredients for the rub and rub three-quarters all over the pork shoulder. Chill for at least 1 hour or up to 24 hours.

2. When you're ready to start cooking, preheat the oven to 200°C/190°C fan/gas mark 6.

3. Place the joint in a baking tray and roast for 20 minutes until lightly browned, then remove the tray from the oven and lower the temperature to 180°C/gas mark 4.

4. Bring the apple juice to the boil in a pan and pour it around the joint. Seal the tray really well with foil and return to the oven to cook for 2½ hours, or even longer, until a fork passes through easily. Do not overcook.

5. Meanwhile, make the barbecue sauce. Heat the oil in a pan over a medium heat and cook the onion, red pepper and garlic for 3 minutes to soften slightly. Add the rest of the ingredients and bring to the boil. Reduce the heat and simmer for 10 minutes to cook and thicken. Keep warm.

6. Once the pork is cooked, take it out of the oven and let it cool slightly. Add any juices to the barbecue sauce.

7. 'Pull' apart the meat into long strands. Place them in a bowl and dust well with the remaining rub, mixing well. Add enough sauce to just coat the meat.

8. Serve in gluten-free buns with coleslaw and more of the barbecue sauce.

simple roast pork with rhubarb ketchup

This very simple recipe really packs a punch, and the rhubarb complements the richness of the pork. In fact, any fruit can be made into ketchup – the secret is to get the balance of sweetness and acidity right.

1 x 4-bone loin of pork (about 2kg), chined, or 1.5kg boned and rolled pork loin, skin scored well
salt and ground black pepper

FOR THE KETCHUP
500g rhubarb, cut into 2cm chunks
100g caster sugar
100ml white wine vinegar
salt and ground black pepper

Serves 4 • **PREP TIME** *15 minutes* • **COOKING TIME** *about 1 hour*

1. Preheat the oven to 200°C/190°C/gas mark 6. Scrunch up a large piece of foil and place it in the centre of a baking tray.

2. Place the pork in the tray, propped up against the foil, and season it really well with salt and pepper. Cook for 20 minutes, then reduce the heat to 180°C and cook for a further 30–40 minutes.

3. Meanwhile, put the rhubarb into a stainless steel pan over a gentle heat. Add 50ml of cold water and cook until you have a thick stew. Blend, then pass through a fine nylon sieve back into the pan.

4. Add the sugar and vinegar, season with salt and pepper, and bring to the boil. Cook down gently for 15–20 minutes until the sauce is a thick consistency similar to double cream.

5. After 30–40 minutes, remove the joint from the oven and turn the heat up to 220°C/gas mark 7. If you're using a tied joint, cut away the strings.

6. Using a long sharp knife, cut the skin away from the fat, as closed as possible to the skin. Wrap the cooked pork in foil and rest for at least 30–40 minutes. Place the skin back on the foil, fatty side up, and return to the oven for around 15 minutes to crisp up nicely, then remove the crackling from the oven.

7. Carve the pork in thick slices and serve with the warm ketchup and crackling.

Brazilian glazed barbecue pork ribs with a tropical fruit salad

1 large rack of pork
 ribs (roughly 750g)
2 x 10g GF pork
 stock cubes
2 bay leaves
a few black peppercorns
salt and ground black pepper
350–400ml boiling water

FOR THE GLAZE
1 medium guava, skin
 and seeds removed
juice of ½ lime
2 tablespoons honey

FOR THE SALAD
1 papaya, chopped
4 passion fruit, chopped
1 ripe avocado, stoned and
 chopped into chunks
1 garlic clove, crushed
juice of ½ lime
a handful of fresh basil and
 coriander leaves, chopped
salt and ground black pepper
extra virgin olive oil
a squeeze of lemon juice
 (optional)

This dish comes from Rio. The Brazilians love their fruit and eat it with everything, so it made sense to cook a lovely rack of ribs with a fruity glaze and serve a tropical fruit salad alongside. The ribs are finished off on the barbecue so that they're deliciously smoky.

Serves 4 · **PREP TIME** *25 minutes* · **COOKING TIME** *about 2 hours*

1. Preheat the oven to 200°C/190°C/gas mark 6.

2. Put the ribs in a deep baking tray and sprinkle over the stock cubes, bay leaves, peppercorns and good few pinches of salt. Partially cover with boiling water, cover with foil and pop into the oven for about 1½ hours until tender, but not falling apart. Remove and cool, then chill well.

3. Meanwhile, heat the barbecue or griddle to moderate and lightly oil the bars or pan.

4. To make the glaze, blend the guava to a paste and add the lime juice and honey. Don't add too much lime or it will be too acidic.

5. Lift the ribs out of the stock and pat dry on kitchen paper, then oil lightly and season well with salt and pepper. Grill or barbecue for 3–4 minutes to get a good colour. Slather over the glaze and cook for a further 4–5 minutes on each side, taking care not to burn the ribs.

6. Place the papaya, passion fruit, and avocado into a bowl. Add the garlic, lime juice and herbs. Season well and drizzle with olive oil and more lime juice to taste.

7. Serve the glazed ribs with the tropical fruit salad.

TIP *When the meat comes out of the oven it should be soft and tender but not falling off the bone. This is essential or you won't be able to pick the ribs off the barbecue. Greasing the ribs and the bars of the barbecue or a griddle pan will stop the meat sticking.*

succulent pork cutlets with summer vegetables & salsa verde

I love salsa verde and could eat it with anything, if I'm being honest. The punchy anchovy flavour with the garlic and basil is just delicious. The quick curing of the cutlets makes a big difference to the end result.

1½ tablespoons salt

1½ tablespoons caster or granulated sugar

4 x 200g pork cutlets, free of skin and bone

200g cooked Jersey Royal or baby new potatoes

150g cooked green beans, cut into 3cm pieces

250g cooked British asparagus, cut into 3cm pieces

2 tablespoons vegetable oil

6 spring onions, sliced diagonally

75g baby spinach leaves

FOR THE SALSA VERDE

4 salted anchovy fillets

2 garlic cloves, chopped

2 bunches of fresh basil leaves

4 heaped tablespoons chopped fresh parsley

1 tablespoon capers, drained

2 teaspoons GF Dijon mustard

a couple of pinches of hot chilli powder

a pinch of salt

120ml extra virgin olive oil

Serves 4 • **PREP TIME** *30 minutes* • **COOKING TIME** *15–20 minutes*

1. In a small bowl, mix together the salt and sugar.

2. Place the cutlets into a china, glass or stainless steel bowl. Spoon over half the sugar and salt mixture and rub it into the chops well. Turn them over and rub the rest in well. Leave for 10 minutes then turn the chops over again and rub well again. You will see a little liquid coming from the chops. Marinate for a further 10 minutes, then rinse under cold water and pat dry with kitchen paper.

3. Meanwhile, cook the vegetables. Simmer the potatoes in salted boiling water until cooked through, then drain well and leave to one side. Bring a separate pan of water to the boil and add the beans and asparagus. Cook for 2 minutes, then drain well and refresh in cold water to stop the cooking and keep the colour. Drain well before using or the dressing will run off and water it down.

4. Next, make the salsa verde by placing all the ingredients, except for the oil, into a food-processor and blending until smooth. Gradually pour in the oil and bring the mixture together.

5. Heat the 2 tablespoons of oil in a frying pan or wok over a medium heat. Place the cutlets in the pan and cook gently for 3–4 minutes, then turn over and cook for a further 2–3 minutes. Do not overcook. Lift out, cover with cling film and leave to rest.

6. In the same pan, sauté the spring onions for 2 minutes, then add the potatoes and warm through for 4–5 minutes, stirring occasionally. Add the beans, asparagus and spinach, and warm through until the spinach wilts. Take the pan off the heat and stir in enough salsa verde to coat the vegetables. Season with a little pepper.

7. Serve the pork cutlets with the warm vegetables and more salsa verde on the side.

simple Thai beef with ginger, chilli & broccoli

Mint and beef aren't often seen together, but I think they make a great combination.

200g GF flat rice noodles

250g broccoli, cut into small florets

2 tablespoons vegetable oil

450g rump steak, cut into 2cm strips, including the fat

salt and ground black pepper

3 garlic cloves, roughly crushed

2 tablespoons finely chopped fresh ginger

1 tablespoon roughly chopped red jalapeño chilli

4 tablespoons GF tamari sauce

2 teaspoons sesame oil

juice of 1 large lime

4 tablespoons chopped fresh mint

4 lime wedges, to serve

Serves 4 · **PREP TIME** *20 minutes* · **COOKING TIME** *15–18 minutes*

1. Place the noodles in a bowl and cover with boiling water. Leave for 15 minutes to soften.

2. Place a pan of cold salted water over a high heat and bring to the boil. Plunge in the broccoli and bring back to the boil, then immediately strain off the water.

3. Heat 1 tablespoon of the oil in a wok or large frying pan over a high heat. Season the steak well and tip half into the hot pan. Cook just until the outside is seared and the meat has a good colour, then spoon onto a plate. Do not overcook. Wipe out the wok with kitchen paper and repeat with the remaining meat.

4. Add the garlic, ginger and chilli to the pan and cook for 1–2 minutes. Add the cooked noodles and beef and stir well. Add the tamari, sesame oil, lime juice and salt and pepper, and cook until the steak is cooked but still nice and pink.

5. Remove the pan from the heat and stir in the cooked broccoli and mint.

6. Serve in deep bowls with the lime wedges.

TIP *A lot of fine rice noodles and vermicelli just need to be soaked in boiling water for 20 minutes to soften, but I have found that for some of the larger, flatter noodles soaking is insufficient and they need a little bit of boiling to soften.*

loaded burgers

Remember, the secrets of a good burger are:

1. Use minced or ground braising steak – 'chuck steak', as the Americans call it. If you're mincing the meat at home, an 8mm mincing plate size is perfect.

2. Use meat that has a minimum of 15 to 20 per cent fat content.

3. Mince the meat twice, then mix it all together well. The burgers will bind more easily and hold their fat and moisture better.

500g beef mince
(15–20 per cent fat content)
3 tablespoons dried natural
GF breadcrumbs
salt and ground black pepper
(optional)
½ red onion, finely sliced
4 tablespoons red wine
vinegar
12 rashers of streaky bacon,
American-style if you can
get them
12 slices cooking chorizo
vegetable oil, for greasing
200g strong Cheddar cheese,
grated
2–3 tablespoons maple syrup
6 large GF burger buns, sliced
in half, to serve

Serves 6 • **PREP TIME** *10 minutes* • **COOKING TIME** *8–10 minutes*

1. Mix together the mince and breadcrumbs. Add salt and pepper if liked. Mould into patties.

2. Soak the onion in the vinegar for 15 minutes to soften.

3. Heat a frying pan over a high heat and cook the bacon rashers. Transfer to a warm plate and reduce the heat to moderate. Lay the chorizo strips in the pan and lightly fry.

4. Heat a griddle or frying pan over a high heat and brush with oil. Alternatively, heat a barbecue and oil the bars.

5. Cook the burgers for 2–3 minutes, then turn them over and cook for a further 2–3 minutes until nice and brown on the outside and just cooked in the middle.

6. Place a burger on a gluten-free bun base and sprinkle with cheese. Lay the chorizo on top, followed by the pickled onion and bacon rashers. Drizzle with maple syrup and top the bun. Serve.

cottage pie

Everyone has a recipe for cottage pie – I love the stuff. There are a couple of things to remember here. As most mince is vacuum-packed, make sure you cook the mince and onions until all the water has evaporated. The meat will boil initially, then start to brown nicely. Secondly, once the meat is cooked, pour it into a dish and cool, or better still, chill until set. This makes sure that when you top it with the mash, it doesn't sink in.

---

4 tablespoons vegetable oil
3 medium onions, diced
500g beef mince
  (15 per cent fat)
3 garlic cloves, crushed
2 tablespoons GF Flour Mix A
  (page 15)
2 tablespoons tomato purée
a pinch of dried thyme
3 tablespoons Worcestershire
  sauce
about 300ml hot GF strong
  beef stock, or 300ml hot
  water and 1 x 10g GF beef
  stock cube
salt and ground black pepper
750g potatoes (Maris Piper,
  Desiree, or similar), peeled
  and chopped into chunks
150ml hot milk
50g butter or 50ml olive oil
a pinch of nutmeg

Serves 4–6 • **PREP TIME** *20 minutes* • **COOKING TIME** *30 minutes*

1. Heat the oil in a large pan over a low heat and cook the onions for 10 minutes until slightly browned. Add the mince, breaking it up well in the pan. Cook until all the moisture has evaporated and the mince starts to brown in the oil and fat from the meat.

2. Add the garlic and gluten-free flour, and mix well to soak up any fat. Continue to cook until the flour browns well on the bottom of the pan. Next, add the tomato purée, thyme, Worcestershire sauce and enough stock to just cover the meat. Season well with salt and pepper, and cook gently for 20–25 minutes, stirring occasionally. Tip the mixture into a baking dish and leave to cool. It should be fairly thick.

3. Meanwhile, cook the potatoes in salted boiling water for 10 minutes until soft, then mash them.

4. Whisk the hot milk, butter or oil and nutmeg into the mashed potatoes and season well with salt and pepper. The mash should be soft but not too creamy.

5. Spoon the mash over the cooled, set mince and fluff it up with a fork.

6. Half an hour before you're ready to serve, reheat the pie in the oven at 180°C/gas mark 4 for 20–25 minutes until golden and slightly crunchy on top.

braised beef cheeks with carrots & onions

This recipe is so simple yet so tasty, and the gravy you get from it is so thick and full of flavour that it also makes a fab meal just poured over rice or potatoes. It does take a few hours to make, and it's one of those dishes that doesn't seem to want to cook for ages, then all of a sudden you have the most moist, succulent, soft, beautiful texture and flavour.

2 large beef cheeks (about 1kg), trimmed

2 large carrots, peeled and roughly chopped

2 large onions, roughly diced

2 teaspoons dried oregano

2 x 10g GF beef stock cubes

4 tablespoons Worcestershire sauce

salt and ground black pepper

2 tablespoons starch, such as cornflour, arrowroot or tapioca (optional)

mashed potato or boiled rice, to serve

Serves 4 • **PREP TIME** *10 minutes* • **COOKING TIME** *about 4 hours*

1. Preheat the oven to 180°C/160°C fan/gas mark 4.

2. Cut each cheek into four pieces, then place in a deep ovenproof pan. Add the carrots, onions and oregano, and cover with cold water. Crumble in the stock cube and add the Worcestershire sauce. Season with salt and pepper, and bring to the boil over a high heat. Cover with a tight-fitting lid.

3. Transfer to the oven and cook for 3½ to 4 hours. Keep checking to avoid overcooking.

4. Once cooked, you may want to thicken the sauce slightly with a little starch and cold water stirred into the simmering stew, but don't go mad.

5. That's it! Serve with mashed potatoes or plain boiled rice.

TIP *For me, cheek is the best cut when it comes to stewing. If you can't get cheeks from your supermarket or butcher, big chunks of chuck steak will work pretty well.*

spicy beef meatballs

500g beef mince
1 small onion, finely diced
1 egg white
2 garlic cloves, crushed
2 teaspoons dried thyme
1 tablespoon tomato purée
2 tablespoons honey
4 tablespoons Worcestershire
    sauce
2 tablespoons unsalted butter
100g spinach
salt and ground black pepper

I once had a version of this dish in Greece. Worcestershire sauce is my addition, as is the spinach. Serve with Simple Braised Rice (page 70) and a spinach salad.

Serves 4 · **PREP TIME** *20 minutes* · **COOKING TIME** *20 minutes*

1. Place the mince, onion, egg white, garlic, thyme, tomato purée, honey and 2 tablespoons of the Worcestershire sauce into a bowl and mix well. Form into about 14–16 small balls.

2. Heat the butter in a frying pan and add the meatballs. Cook for about 10 minutes, turning to make sure they're cooked and nicely browned all over. Transfer to a warm plate.

3. Add the spinach to the pan with the remaining Worcestershire sauce and cook until wilted. Return the meatballs to the pan, coat them well, season and serve.

char siu pork

2–3 tablespoons vegetable oil
2 small onions, finely chopped
4 garlic cloves, finely chopped
2 tablespoons chopped
    fresh ginger
150ml GF tamari sauce
4 tablespoons GF smooth
    peanut butter
4 tablespoons GF tomato
    ketchup
2 tablespoons clear honey
2 tablespoons sesame oil
2 tablespoons cider vinegar
½ teaspoon dried chilli flakes
500–600g roasted shoulder or
    pork, the fattier the better,
    cut into 3cm pieces

Traditional char siu is slowly grilled or barbecued marinated pork, although there are many different twists on it. This is my not quite authentic version, which I find is better made with leftover roast shoulder of pork.

Serves 4 · **PREP TIME** *25 minutes* · **COOKING TIME** *20 minutes*

1. Heat the oil in a large, shallow pan, add the onions, garlic and ginger, and cook for 10 minutes to soften slightly. Add the remaining ingredients, except for the meat, stir well, then bring to a simmer.

2. Once simmering, add the pork and coat it well in the sauce. Continue to simmer for 10 minutes to warm the pork through, stirring every few minutes. The sauce should end up coating the cooked pork. Serve with rice noodles or plain boiled rice.

rose veal, Parmesan & lemon meatballs

Rose veal has become increasingly popular over the past few years, primarily because welfare standards have improved and the young animals now live outdoors for up to a year. The meat is delicious, with very little fat and a lovely colour. This recipe is based on a dish I once had in Italy. It also works well with minced pork, chicken, turkey and even pheasant.

500g rose veal mince
2 small onions, finely diced
4 garlic cloves
zest of 2 lemons
50g Parmesan cheese, finely
    grated
50g fresh basil, chopped
salt and ground black pepper

FOR THE SAUCE
2 tablespoons olive oil
2 medium onions, diced
2 garlic cloves, finely chopped
150g soft cooking chorizo,
    cut into very small pieces
500ml passata
a pinch of sugar
finely grated zest and juice
    of 1 large lemon
salt and ground black pepper

Serves 4 • **PREP TIME** *25 minutes* • **COOKING TIME** *40–50 minutes*

1. Preheat the oven to 200°C/190°C fan/gas mark 6.

2. In a bowl, mix together the veal, onions, garlic, lemon zest, Parmesan and basil, and season well with salt and pepper. Roll the mixture into balls about the size of a walnut.

3. To make the sauce, heat the oil in a deep ovenproof pan. Cook the onions, garlic and chorizo for 4–5 minutes until the colour is released from the chorizo. Add the passata, sugar, lemon juice and zest, season with salt and pepper and bring to the boil.

4. Reduce the heat to a simmer and add the meatballs, covering them with the sauce, then cover the pan and transfer to the oven. Cook for 35–40 minutes.

5. Serve in deep bowls with a simple green salad.

desserts

fluffy thick pancakes with buttery pears, almonds & orange

These fluffy white pancakes are delicious and the buttery poached pears combined with the orange zest are the ideal accompaniment. Toasted flaked almonds add a nice crunch.

100g flaked almonds
115g GF fine rice flour
½ teaspoon GF baking powder
a pinch of salt
1 medium egg
1½ tablespoons sunflower oil
300ml buttermilk
3 tablespoons olive oil
75g salted butter, cubed
2 ripe William pears, peeled, cored and sliced into 8 long shards each
4 tablespoons vanilla sugar
finely grated zest and juice of 2 large oranges
GF vanilla ice cream, to serve

Serves 4 · **PREP TIME** *15 minutes* · **COOKING TIME** *25 minutes*

1. Heat a dry non-stick pan over a medium heat and toast the almonds for a few minutes until lightly browned.

2. Place the rice flour, baking powder and salt in a bowl.

3. In a separate bowl, whisk together the egg, sunflower oil and buttermilk.

4. Gradually add the wet mix to the dry mix. You should end up with a loose, but thickish batter.

5. Heat the olive oil in a large non-stick frying pan. Spoon a ladleful of the pancake mixture into the pan and swirl it around to make a thin pancake. Cook for 2–3 minutes until the edges are cooked and the bottom of the pancake is lightly browned. Flip over and cook the other side. Repeat until you have six to eight small pancakes. Keep warm.

6. Meanwhile, melt the butter in a pan. When the butter is foaming, add the pear slices and quickly warm through. Add the sugar and orange zest, and toss to cover the pancakes. Finally, add the orange juice and almonds, and cook until slightly thickened.

7. Lay the pancakes on warm plates and quickly spoon the pear mixture over the warm pancakes. Serve with soft gluten-free vanilla ice cream.

chocolate profiteroles

These profiteroles, which can also be made as éclairs, are wheat and gluten free. Halve the quantities if you would like to make less.

---

1 quantity Choux Pastry
  (page 47)
1 quantity Chocolate Glacé
  Icing (page 227)

FOR THE FILLING
500ml double cream, softly
  whipped

Makes about 50 profiteroles or 25 éclairs · **PREP TIME** *25 minutes* · **COOKING TIME** *25–30 minutes*

1. Preheat the oven to 220°C/200°C fan/gas mark 7. Line two baking trays with greaseproof paper and brush with oil.

2. Fit a wide, plain piping nozzle in a large piping bag and fill with the choux pastry, while still warm. Pipe small balls, or 10cm long shapes for éclairs, onto the trays. Space them evenly apart and try to pipe them all the same size.

3. Place the trays in the preheated oven and bake for 25–30 minutes until well risen and nicely coloured.

4. Check on the choux pastries while they are cooking: you may need to turn the trays to ensure even browning, or move them to a different shelf.

5. Just when you think they are cooked, give them an extra 5 minutes to dry the inside nicely. There shouldn't be any white part visible near the bottom of the pastry. Remove from the oven and cool.

6. When cold, fill a piping bag with the cream, push the nozzle into each choux pastry shell and fill with the cream. Finally top each pastry with chocolate fondant icing: spoon the icing on top and leave to set. Keep the profiteroles in the fridge.

apple Calvados cheesecake

This is a very light cheesecake that's easy to make. The brandy really gives the dessert a lift. I use gluten-free shortbread, but any gluten-free biscuit or cookie will do.

Serves 8–10 • **PREP TIME** *25 minutes* • **CHILLING TIME** *4 hours or overnight*

butter, for greasing
2 medium Bramley or other
    cooking apples
100g caster or granulated
    sugar
100ml Calvados or other
    brandy
200g GF Shortbread (page
    211), crushed with
    a rolling pin
75g dark GF chocolate, melted
400g tin condensed milk
500g mascarpone cheese
juice of 3 large lemons
    (about 100ml)
icing sugar, to dust
whipped cream, to serve

FOR THE APPLE AND LIME
SYRUP TOPPING
1 medium Bramley or other
    cooking apple, peeled and
    finely chopped
225g caster or granulated
    sugar
juice and finely grated zest
    of 3 large limes

1. Grease a 20cm spring-form cake tin and line the base with baking parchment.

2. To make the sauce, place the apple and sugar in a pan with 250ml of cold water and cook gently until you have a soft, thin purée. Blitz in a blender for a good 5 minutes until you have a velvety, smooth sauce. Pass through a fine sieve into a bowl and leave to cool, then add the lime juice and zest and stir in well.

3. Peel and core the apples. Place in a pan with the sugar and Calvados, and cook until you have a thick pulp – the thicker the better. Leave to cool.

4. Meanwhile, in a bowl mix together the crushed shortbread and melted chocolate, then lightly press the mixture into the base of the tin to make an even layer. Chill for 20 minutes.

5. Use an electric whisk to beat the condensed milk with the mascarpone until the mixture is smooth. Add the lemon juice and combine thoroughly.

6. Spread half the mascarpone mixture onto the biscuit base. Spoon about half the stewed apples over the top, leaving a 3cm gap around the edge. Top with the remaining mascarpone mixture, covering the edges to seal in the apple stew. Chill for 4–8 hours or preferably overnight.

7. Once chilled, place the tin on a plate and spoon the rest of the apple stew over the centre of the cheesecake, carefully spreading it out but keeping a 3cm gap around the edge.

8. Dust heavily with icing sugar and serve in wedges with the sauce and thickly whipped cream on the side.

chocolate mousse tart

This is such a simple recipe but results in a wonderful taste and texture. The secret is not to over-fold the chocolate into the butter and, once cooked, to leave the tart to set at room temperature before cutting. Don't put it in the fridge.

150g GF bitter chocolate
150g GF milk chocolate
2 medium eggs, plus
  2 medium egg yolks,
  at room temperature
60g caster sugar
130g salted butter, melted
1 x 23cm x 3cm-deep blind-
  baked tart case using the
  Chocolate Shortcrust Pastry
  (pages 43 and 17)
icing sugar, to dust
Fresh Raspberry Sauce
  (page 201), to serve

Makes 23cm x 3cm-deep tart · **PREP TIME** *25 minutes*
· **COOKING TIME** *20 minutes in total*

1. Preheat the oven to 220°C/200°C fan/gas mark 7.

2. Place a heatproof bowl over a pan of gently simmering water. The base of the bowl must not touch the water. Break both types of chocolate into the bowl and melt together.

3. Place the eggs, yolks and sugar into a separate bowl and whisk at high speed until very thick; this will take about 6–8 minutes.

4. Carefully stir in the melted chocolate, taking care not to knock too much air from the eggs. Finally, fold in the melted butter, again very carefully. It will seem like it's not folding in, but just be patient.

5. Pour the mixture into the pastry case and bake for 8 minutes to just set. Don't let the edges of the tart start to rise. Remove from the oven and cool on a wire rack.

6. Dust heavily with icing sugar. Serve at room temperature, sliced into wedges, with a little fresh raspberry sauce on the side.

easy iced peanut butter mousse

If you love peanut butter, then you'll be in heaven here. Chill well and store in the fridge.

8 heaped tablespoons GF
   smooth peanut butter
300g GF milk chocolate
55g GF puffed rice cereal,
   lightly crushed
a pinch of salt
150ml milk
200ml double cream
Fresh Raspberry Sauce
   (page 201), to serve

Serves 6 • **PREP TIME** *15 minutes* • **COOKING TIME** *10 minutes*

1. Put 5 heaped tablespoons of the peanut butter and 70g of the chocolate in a heatproof bowl. Melt together in the microwave in short 30-second bursts, or over a pan of simmering water, making sure the base of the bowl doesn't touch the water.

2. Add the puffed rice to the peanut chocolate mixture, then spoon onto a sheet of baking paper and spread out to an even 1cm layer. Lay a second piece of paper over the top and roll out until nice and thin, about 5mm. Freeze.

3. Grease a 1lb loaf tin and line it with cling film.

4. To make the mousse, melt the remaining chocolate, peanut butter and salt together either in the microwave or over simmering water, as before.

5. Put a pan over a medium heat and bring the milk to a simmer, then carefully pour over the chocolate and peanut mixture. Whisk well to combine.

6. Transfer the mixture to a stand mixer and continue to whisk until light, thick and completely cold. Lightly whip the cream and gently fold it into the mixture, then spoon the whole thing into the lined loaf tin. Cover with cling film and freeze overnight.

7. When you're ready to serve, carefully turn out the mousse from the tin and take off the cling film. Take the chocolate rice biscuit out of the freezer and cut it into shards.

8. Slice the mousse and serve with a shard of the rice biscuit and a spoonful of raspberry sauce.

meringues

The three things to remember about egg whites when making meringue are:

1. Always start with your eggs at room temperature. This helps to whip in the air, as the bubbles are a lot more stretchy.

2. If you're using a stand mixer, always whisk at no more than three-quarters of the maximum speed. This will produce a soft, shiny meringue, ideal for soufflés and piping.

3. Always weigh the egg whites, then allow double the amount of sugar, so 100g egg white would require 200g sugar. Using half caster and half sieved icing sugar gives you a softer, smoother meringue.

---

2 large egg whites (70g),
 at room temperature
a pinch of cream of tartar
70g caster sugar
70g icing sugar, sieved
2–3 tablespoons freeze-dried
 fruit powder (optional)

Makes 10–12 · **PREP TIME** *10 minutes*
· **COOKING TIME** *about 2 hours*

1. Preheat the oven to 140°C/gas mark 1 and the same for a fan oven. Line two baking sheets with baking paper.

2. Place the egg whites and cream of tartar into the bowl of a mixer and whisk on a medium to high speed until thick and creamy, but not grainy. Add the caster sugar and whisk until firm, but silky and shiny.

3. Remove the bowl from the mixer and carefully fold in the sieved icing sugar and any fruit powder, if using.

4. Spoon or pipe small mounds of meringues evenly onto the prepared baking sheet. Each one should be about the size of a small scone. Bake for 2 hours or until dried out completely.

TIP *Freeze-dried fruit powders are now available in lots of shops and supermarkets. They're great for colouring meringues.*

chilled crème fraîche rice with medjool dates, honey & toasted almonds

When it comes to puddings, there's nothing quite like medjool dates to add texture and a rich toffee caramel flavour; they're good in pretty much any pud. Warming them slightly and serving them with crème fraîche makes them even better. This pudding can be served hot, warm or chilled.

100g flaked almonds
600ml milk
1 vanilla pod, split
55g short-grain pudding rice
125g golden caster sugar
250g soft, medjool dates,
    cut into small chunks
100ml double cream
250g thick crème fraîche
juice of 1 large lemon

Serves 4 · **PREP TIME** *15 minutes* · **COOKING TIME** *40 minutes*

1. Preheat the oven to 150°C/140°C fan/gas mark 2.

2. Heat a dry non-stick pan over a medium heat and toast the almonds for a few minutes until lightly brown.

3. Bring the milk and vanilla pod to the boil in an ovenproof pan over a high heat. Add the rice and stir well, cover and place in the oven for 40–50 minutes, or until thick and creamy.

4. Once the rice is cooked, remove it from the oven and stir in the sugar and dates, then cover and cool. Once cooled chill in the refrigerator.

5. When you're ready to serve, spoon the chilled rice into a large bowl and break up with a wooden spoon. Add the cream, crème fraîche and lemon juice, and mix well. Finally, stir in the almonds and serve.

honey, pear & pecan meringue cake with salted caramel sauce

This decadent dessert never fails to impress and is very easy to make. I even use tinned pears for convenience but you can, of course, poach fresh ones. I sometimes also use tinned peaches, for added colour.

4 medium egg whites (200g), at room temperature

a pinch of cream of tartar

200g caster sugar

1 teaspoon cornflour

3–4 teaspoons vanilla essence

1 teaspoon white wine vinegar

150g pecan nuts, roughly chopped

4 tablespoons clear honey

750ml double cream, plus 175ml for topping

2 x 410g tins pears, drained and sliced lengthways

icing sugar, for dusting

FOR THE CARAMEL SAUCE

175g soft brown sugar

200ml whipping cream

100g salted butter, cut into small cubes

a pinch of salt (optional)

Serves 6–8 • **PREP TIME** *35 minutes* • **COOKING TIME** *1 hour 20 minutes*

1. Preheat the oven to 120°C/gas mark ½. Line a Swiss roll tin with baking paper.

2. Place the egg whites and cream of tartar into the bowl of a mixer and whisk until light and foamy. Add half the sugar and whisk well on a medium speed, until thick and glossy but not overbeaten. If you over-whisk, the meringue will be dull and firm. Add the rest of the sugar and just bring together for about 2 minutes.

3. Remove the bowl from the mixer and fold in the cornflour, 1 teaspoon of the vanilla essence and the vinegar, and mix well. Spread the mixture onto the prepared tin and bake for 1 hour 15 minutes, then remove from the oven and cool slightly. Cut the meringue into three even-sized pieces and leave to cool completely.

4. Meanwhile, make the salted caramel sauce. Place the sugar in a pan and just cover with cold water. Bring to the boil and cook until all the water has evaporated and you're left with a brown caramel. Carefully add the cream, butter and salt, if using, standing back as the caramel may spit, and stir well until all incorporated. Chill.

5. Heat a dry non-stick pan and gently toast the pecans. When nicely browned, tip into a bowl, add the honey and mix well.

6. Whip together the cream and remaining vanilla until glossy and soft. Quickly spread half the whipped cream over one of the meringue pieces. Lay the sliced pears on top. Sprinkle over one-third of the honeyed pecans and drizzle with a little of the salted caramel sauce. Place a second meringue on top and repeat, finishing with the last meringue layer. Gently but firmly press down on the cake using a cooling rack to ensure the layers are even.

7. Decorate the top of the cake with the remaining piped cream, slices of pear and the remaining pecans. Dust well with icing sugar.

8. Just before serving, drizzle over a little more caramel sauce and dust well with icing sugar. Slice and serve with extra sauce.

passion fruit pavlova

Pavlova is one of the most delicious desserts ever invented and works well with any fruit or fruit combination. A soft marshmallow-like centre is essential. Once the meringue is just cooked, my mother turns off the oven and leaves it to cool overnight in the oven. I'm certainly not going to argue with her. I sometimes serve it topped with a ball of dark fruit sorbet. It will keep in the fridge for 2–3 hours.

4 medium egg whites (200g), at room temperature
a pinch of cream of tartar
400g caster sugar
1 teaspoon cornflour
1 teaspoon vanilla extract
1 teaspoon white wine vinegar

FOR THE FILLING
10 ripe passion fruit, halved and seeds scooped out
55g golden caster sugar
finely grated zest of 1 large lemon
600ml double cream, very lightly whipped

Serves 8 • **PREP TIME** *10 minutes, plus overnight cooling* • **COOKING TIME** *1 hour 15 minutes*

1. Preheat the oven to 120°C/gas mark ½, and the same for fan ovens. Using a dinner or side plate as a template, draw a 20cm circle in the centre of a sheet of baking paper.

2. Place the egg whites and cream of tartar into the bowl of a mixer and whisk until light and foamy. Add half the sugar and whisk well on a medium to three-quarter speed, until thick and glossy but not overbeaten. If you over-whisk, the meringue will be dull and firm. Add the rest of the sugar and whisk until very glossy. Remove the bowl from the machine and fold in the cornflour, vanilla and vinegar.

3. Place the baking paper on a baking sheet, drawn side face down (you should be able to see the circle through the paper). Spoon the meringue into the centre of the circle and, using a palette knife or the back of a large spoon, carefully spread it to the edge of the circle. Build up the edges so that they're nice and high (remember this will eventually hold a lot of passion fruit and cream).

4. Bake for about 1 hour 15 minutes. The meringue will expand quite a lot, slightly colour and crack; this is normal. Check it after 1 hour: it should be firm to the touch, yet crack if squeezed lightly. If not, leave it for a bit longer. Once cooked, turn off the heat and leave the meringue in the oven to cool for a few hours or overnight.

5. In a bowl, fold the seeds and pulp from 8 of the passion fruit, the sugar and lemon zest into the cream, making sure not to over-mix. The acid from the passion fruit will thicken the cream and you'll have a pretty swirled effect. Spoon into the meringue nest and pile high, then chill well for 30 minutes.

6. To serve, dust with icing sugar and spoon over the seeds and pulp from the remaining passion fruit.

raspberry & blueberry cheesecake pavlova

This is another twist on a regular pavlova, and is equally delicious.
If you can make it and then leave it to chill in the fridge for 1 hour
– it will be all the better for it.

4 medium egg whites (200g),
   at room temperature
a pinch of cream of tartar
400g caster sugar
1 teaspoon cornflour
2 teaspoons vanilla extract
1 teaspoon balsamic vinegar
200g full-fat soft cheese
400g tin condensed milk
100g fresh blueberries
100g frozen raspberries,
   defrosted
finely grated zest and juice
   of 2 large lemons
icing sugar, to dust
Fresh Raspberry Sauce (page
   201), to serve
thick pouring cream and/or
   GF vanilla ice cream, to serve

Serves 8 · **PREP TIME** *10 minutes* · **COOKING TIME** *10–12 minutes*

1. Preheat the oven to 120°C/gas mark ½, and the same for fan ovens. Using a bowl or side plate as a template, draw two 15cm circles on a sheet of baking paper.

2. Place the egg whites and cream of tartar into the bowl of a mixer and whisk until light and foamy. Add half the sugar and whisk well on a medium to three-quarter speed, until thick and glossy but not overbeaten. If you over-whisk, the meringue will be dull and firm. Add the rest of the sugar and whisk until very glossy. Remove the bowl from the machine and fold in the cornflour, vanilla and vinegar.

3. Place the baking paper on a baking sheet, drawn side face down (you should be able to see the circles through the paper). Spoon the meringue evenly into the centre of the circles and, using a palette knife or the back of a large spoon, carefully spread to the edge of the circles.

4. Bake for about 1 hour 15 minutes. The meringue will expand quite a lot, slightly colour and crack; this is normal. Check it after 1 hour: it should be firm to the touch, yet crack if squeezed lightly. If not, leave it for a bit longer. Once cooked, turn off the heat and leave the meringue in the oven to cool for a few hours or overnight.

5. In a bowl, whisk together the soft cheese and condensed milk for 10 minutes. Add the fruit and any liquid from the raspberries, and mix well. Finally, add the lemon juice and zest and gently mix in.

6. Place one of the meringue layers onto a serving plate and spoon the filling into the centre. Top with the second meringue layer. Dust with icing sugar and chill for 1 hour in the fridge.

7. Cut and serve with raspberry sauce, thick pouring cream and/or a ball of gluten-free vanilla ice cream.

fresh strawberry sauce

250g ripe strawberries
50–60g caster sugar
2 tablespoons lemon juice
1 tablespoon strawberry jam
(optional)

The secret to this sauce are the strawberries: they need to be ripe and perfumed. If your fruit isn't sweet, add more sugar; if it's bland, add a little strawberry jam – you'll be surprised the impact a small amount can have. I have purposely left the quantities a little vague, as the taste and consistency are really up to you.

Makes 4 servings • **PREP TIME** *10 minutes*

1. Wash the strawberries well, then hull them. Pop them into a blender along with 50g of the sugar, the lemon juice, jam, if using, and a little cold water, and blitz until you have a smooth sauce.

2. Strain into a bowl through a fine sieve and add more sugar, to taste. Do not over-sweeten. Keep refrigerated for up to three days.

fresh raspberry sauce

This is a great sauce for meringues, pavlovas, pancakes or just over ice cream or sorbet. I find frozen raspberries make a deeper-coloured and flavoured sauce. Adjust the sugar according to the sweetness of the raspberries.

225g fresh or good-quality
    frozen raspberries
about 100g caster sugar
1 tablespoon lemon juice

Makes about 200g • **PREP TIME** *10 minutes*

Place the raspberries in a blender along with the sugar and lemon juice, and blend until smooth. You may need to add a touch of cold water if the sauce is too thick. Pass through a fine sieve. Keep refrigerated for up to three days.

dairy-free & gluten-free bitter chocolate sauce

I once had a bitter chocolate soufflé in Florence that was flavoured with olive oil. When it came to the table, the aroma was something I will never forget. A little of the best-quality extra virgin oil you can find in this sauce sets it off perfectly. I use this sauce cold (without oil) to pour over profiteroles; it has a wonderful shine.

175g cocoa powder
175g caster sugar
2 tablespoons best-quality
    extra virgin olive oil
    (optional)

Makes 500ml • **PREP TIME** *5 minutes* • **COOKING TIME** *5 minutes*

1. Place the cocoa powder, sugar and 600ml of cold water into a pan over a high heat and bring to the boil. Cook for 1 minute.

2. Take the pan off the heat and whisk in the oil, if using. Serve hot or cold. Keep for up to two weeks in the fridge.

simple coffee custard

The secret to this very simple sauce is to use good-quality freshly ground coffee. It's lovely served with ice cream, chocolate tart or mousse.

500ml milk
75g good-quality freshly
    ground coffee beans
5 medium egg yolks
100g caster sugar

Serves 4 • **PREP TIME** *10 minutes* • **COOKING TIME** *10 minutes*

1. Put a pan over a medium heat and bring the milk and coffee to a simmer, then remove from the heat to infuse for 10 minutes.

2. In a bowl, whisk together the egg yolks and sugar for 3–4 minutes. The more creamy and frothy the egg and sugar mixture is, the thicker the sauce will be. Pour over the hot coffee milk, whisk well, then return to the pan.

3. Cook over a very low heat until the mixture is thick and glossy. Strain through a fine sieve, cool and chill. Keeps for up to three days in the fridge.

crème fraîche

Many years ago I made crème fraîche using raw, unpasteurised double cream. It was so good – thick with a lovely sharp edge. Nowadays, I use regular double cream and it works very well. Make sure everything is spotlessly clean and all your equipment has been sterilised, either with boiling water or run through the dishwasher.

600ml really fresh double
    cream
110ml buttermilk

Makes 600ml • **PREP TIME** *20 minutes* • **COOKING TIME** *5 minutes*

1. Heat the cream to 90°C in a heavy-based pan over a high heat, then take off the heat and leave to cool for about 15–20 minutes.

2. Whisk in the buttermilk and pour into a very clean bowl. Cover with cling film and leave in a warm place for 24–48 hours. The cream will thicken considerably.

3. Once thickened, chill really well, overnight if possible. Use the same day.

easy syrup sponges

I use a 700 watt microwave and cook small items on full power. If you're making a single large sponge, then cook on three-quarter power as the mixture will be slightly more dense. Keep an eye on large mixes – you will sometimes find that the bottom of the sponge will still be undercooked, even if the top is very firm. You may need to add a minute or two extra to the cooking time. Another good rule of thumb is to leave the sponge to rest once cooked for the same length of time you cooked it, still wrapped well in the cling film.

150g margarine, at room
　temperature, plus
　2 tablespoons, melted
4 tablespoons golden syrup
100g GF fine white rice flour
50g GF potato flour
1 teaspoon GF baking powder
150g caster sugar
2 teaspoons vanilla extract
2 medium eggs, at room
　temperature
custard, cream or GF ice cream,
　to serve

Serves 4 • **PREP TIME** *15 minutes* • **COOKING TIME** *3 minutes*

1. Grease four 8cm round x 5.5cm high microwavable bowls well with the melted margarine, and spoon 1 tablespoon of golden syrup into the bottom of each one.

2. In a separate bowl, mix together the rice flour, potato flour and baking powder.

3. Place the rest of the margarine, the sugar and vanilla into a mixing bowl or the bowl of a stand mixer. Whisk on a high speed or with an electric hand whisk for 2 minutes, then stop whisking and add the eggs and the flour mixture. Whisk again for 20 seconds in the mixer, or a few seconds more if whisking by hand, until incorporated.

4. Spoon the mixture evenly between the four bowls, over the golden syrup. Cover each one loosely with cling film and make a small incision in the film to let the steam escape.

5. Microwave on high for 3 minutes, then carefully remove the very hot bowls and leave to stand for 2 minutes to set.

6. Remove the cling film and turn the puddings out into bowls. You will see a small cracking in the top, but this is quite normal. Serve topped with custard, cream or gluten-free ice cream.

TIP *If you're not eating the puddings immediately, leave the cling film over the top to stop the sponges drying out.*

cookies, cakes & muffins

chocolate chip cookies

These cookies have just the right texture: crisp on the outside and slightly soft in the centre. The longer you cook them, the crispier they'll be. This recipe is gluten, wheat, dairy and egg free, but you can use butter if you prefer. Store in an airtight container.

140g GF Sorghum Flour Mix (page 14)

¼ level teaspoon xanthan gum

1 teaspoon bicarbonate of soda

50g dark soft brown sugar

25g GF dairy-free dark chocolate chips

85g maple syrup

50g dairy-free margarine, melted

½ teaspoon vanilla extract or paste

1 teaspoon blackstrap molasses or treacle

Makes 12 large or 20 small · **PREP TIME** *10 minutes* · **COOKING TIME** *15 minutes*

1. Preheat the oven to 190°C/180°C fan/gas mark 5. Line a baking sheet with baking paper.

2. In a large bowl, sift together the gluten-free flour, xanthan gum and bicarbonate of soda; be sure to mix evenly and thoroughly. Stir in the sugar, breaking up any lumps. Add the chocolate chips.

3. In a small bowl, combine the maple syrup, melted margarine, vanilla and molasses or treacle, then spoon the wet ingredients into the dry mixture and stir until just combined and evenly mixed. Don't over-beat the mixture.

4. Divide into 12 balls, or 20 if you like mini cookies, and space them a few centimetres apart on the prepared baking sheet. Flatten each ball lightly.

5. Bake in the centre of the oven for 10–15 minutes. Cool for a few minutes on the tray before transferring to a wire rack to cool completely.

TRY THIS *Make Pecan and White Chocolate Cookies by substituting chopped pecans, or half pecans and half gluten-free white chocolate, for the chocolate chips. Both types of cookies can be frozen and defrosted at room temperature when you want to eat them. Warm them briefly in a microwave or oven before serving. You can also try this recipe with the GF White and Brown Rice Flour Mix (see page 15)*

maple & pecan cookie creams

This is another recipe that can be dairy free. Any nuts will work – I sometimes use pine nuts for a different texture.

150g GF Sorghum Flour Blend
    or GF Flour Mix B (page 15)
¼ teaspoon GF baking powder
¼ level teaspoon xanthan gum
25g pecans, chopped
50g baking margarine
    or butter
85g dark brown sugar
1 teaspoon vanilla extract
1 medium egg
2 tablespoons maple syrup
25ml milk, or GF dairy-free
    alternative

FOR THE FILLING
150ml double cream, or
    a GF dairy-free alternative
1 tablespoon icing sugar,
    sieved
2 tablespoons maple syrup

Makes 8 sandwiched biscuits • **PREP TIME** *10 minutes* • **COOKING TIME** *15 minutes*

1. Preheat the oven to 190°C/180°C fan/gas mark 5. Line two baking sheets with baking paper.

2. Sift the gluten-free flour, baking powder and xanthan gum into a bowl, then stir in the pecans.

3. In a separate bowl, use an electric whisk to beat the margarine, sugar, vanilla, egg and the maple syrup. Don't worry if the mixture curdles a little.

4. Mix a little of the flour mixture into the creamed mixture, then a little of the milk. Keep alternating until all the flour mixture and milk are added, beating continuously until smooth.

5. Pipe or spoon 16 rounds of the mixture onto the prepared baking sheets, spaced a few centimetres apart, and flatten each round slightly with wet fingers. They should be about 5cm wide. Bake for about 15 minutes until firm. Remove and cool.

6. Whip the cream for the filling until soft, lightly thickened and just holding its shape. Fold in the icing sugar and maple syrup.

7. Spread the filling over the flat sides of half the cookies and sandwich with the other half. Serve the same day, or freeze the cooled biscuits without the filling.

NOTE *See page 239 for more dairy-free filling recipes.*

shortcake biscuits

This rich, buttery shortcake is best eaten on the same day and is especially lovely served with fresh strawberries and whipped cream.

175g GF White and Brown Rice Flour Blend (page 15)
a pinch of salt
¼ level teaspoon xanthan gum
scant 1 teaspoon GF baking powder
50g icing sugar, plus extra for dusting
75g cold unsalted butter, cut into pieces
1 small egg
1 teaspoon vanilla

Makes 20 · **PREP TIME** *10 minutes* · **COOKING TIME** *12–15 minutes*

1. Put the flour, salt, xanthan gum, baking powder, sugar and butter into a food-processor and pulse until the mixture looks like a fine powder. Add the egg and vanilla, and pulse until the mixture starts to clump together; it should be quite soft. If you don't have a food-processor, do this in a large bowl using a wooden spoon.

2. Tip the pastry onto a sheet of cling film and lay another sheet over the top. Roll out to a thin disc no more than 5mm thick. Chill in the cling film for 15 minutes.

3. Preheat the oven to 190°C/180°C fan/gas mark 5. Line a large baking sheet with baking paper.

4. Dip a 5cm cookie cutter in gluten-free flour and cut out the biscuits while the dough is still on the cling film. Don't twist the cutter or the biscuits may rise unevenly. Try not to handle the shapes – use the cling film to help transfer them from the cutter to the baking sheet, leaving a gap between each one. Re-roll and cut any trimmings until all the dough is used up.

5. Bake for 12–15 minutes until, pale and lightly golden. Cool and dust with icing sugar before serving the same day.

NOTE *Cut a small circle from the centre of the biscuits to make rings. Top with an icing of your choice (see pages 236–239 for inspiration) to make party biscuits.*

shortbread

You can make many variations on these biscuits: add a few chocolate chips, or flavour with a pinch of cardamom or little bits of lavender flowers. I find a cooler oven temperature and longer baking time gives the best results. The thicker the biscuits, the longer they will take to bake right through, which is essential for crisp shortbread.

200g GF Flour Mix B (page 15)
a pinch of salt
¼ level teaspoon xanthan gum
50g caster sugar
50g icing sugar
125g very cold unsalted
  butter, cubed
demerara sugar, for sprinkling

Makes 12 fingers • **PREP TIME** *10 minutes* • **COOKING TIME** *45–50 minutes*

1. Line a 20cm square tin with baking paper.

2. In a bowl, mix together the gluten-free flour, salt, xanthan gum and caster and icing sugars, then tip the mixture into a food-processor along with the butter. Pulse until the mixture looks a little like damp sand clumping together. Tip back into the bowl and squeeze lightly to form a loose dough.

3. Tip the pastry onto a sheet of cling film and shape it into a small rectangle. Lay another sheet of cling film over the top and roll out the pastry to about 2cm thick. Cut into fingers and pack closely together in the baking tin. Chill for 30 minutes or overnight.

4. Preheat the oven to 160°C/160°C fan/gas mark 3 and bake the shortbreads for about 45 minutes, or until golden and baked through. The fingers will melt slightly into each other.

5. Score the tops of the biscuits as soon as they come out of the oven. Sprinkle with demerara sugar and leave to cool and harden completely in the tin. Store in an airtight container. Best eaten fresh.

TIP *To make a shortbread case for another recipe, like cheesecake, press the dough crumbs lightly into the base of a lined, loose-based baking tin and bake blind until pale golden.*

dark chocolate, date & fig muffins

These decadent muffins are packed full of flavour, with a texture like a soft and chewy meringue cake. As they're very sweet, make them in cupcake cases rather than large muffin cases.

75g egg whites, at
    room temperature
a pinch of cream of tartar
150g caster sugar
50g GF Flour Mix B (page 15)
100g ground almonds
100g GF dark chocolate,
    finely chopped
75g medjool dates, roughly
    chopped
75g semi-dried figs, roughly
    chopped

FOR THE CHOCOLATE ICING
250g GF dark chocolate
    (70 per cent cocoa solids)
100g salted butter

Makes 12 mini muffins · **PREP TIME** *25 minutes* · **COOKING TIME** *20–25 minutes*

1. Preheat the oven to 190°C/180°C/gas mark 5. Line a 12-hole cupcake tray with paper cases.

2. In a clean bowl whisk the egg whites and cream of tartar for 2 minutes until thick and foamy. Gradually add the sugar and whisk until thick and shiny, as if you were making a meringue.

3. In a separate bowl, mix together the gluten-free flour, ground almonds, chocolate and fruit. Carefully fold into the whisked eggs without losing too much air.

4. Spoon the mixture evenly into the cupcake cases and bake for 20–25 minutes until well risen and firm. Cool on a wire rack.

5. Meanwhile, make the icing. Carefully melt the chocolate with the butter in a heatproof bowl over a pan of gently simmering water. Make sure the base of the bowl doesn't touch the water. Once melted, beat together gently, then leave to cool and thicken to room temperature. Beat gently to form soft peaks, then ice the cooled muffins.

apple & cinnamon muffins

These muffins are as good as the ones you find in cafés, only gluten and wheat free. Don't be tempted to beat the batter.

175g GF Sorghum Flour Blend (page 15)
½ level teaspoon xanthan gum
1 level teaspoon bicarbonate of soda
2 level teaspoons GF baking powder
1 level teaspoon ground cinnamon
¼ teaspoon allspice or grated nutmeg
100g caster sugar
75g dark soft brown sugar
3 medium eggs, at room temperature
4 tablespoons vegetable oil or melted coconut oil
125ml milk, or GF dairy-free alternative
100g GF unsweetened apple sauce
1 teaspoon vanilla extract

Makes 8 large or 12 small • **PREP TIME** *15 minutes* • **COOKING TIME** *20 minutes*

1. Preheat the oven to 190°C/180°C fan/gas mark 5. Line an 8-hole muffin tray with paper cases.

2. In a large bowl, sift the flour with the xanthan gum, bicarbonate of soda, baking powder and spices. Stir in the sugars, breaking up any lumps.

3. In a small bowl, beat the eggs, oil, milk, apple sauce and vanilla until combined.

4. Fold the wet mixture into the dry ingredients and stir until combined. Don't beat. The batter will be really thin and quite wet.

5. Pour the mixture evenly between the muffin cases. Bake for about 20 minutes, or until the surface springs back to the touch. Remove from the oven and leave to cool slightly in the tray before transferring to a wire rack to cool completely.

TIP *Use this mixture to make a small, 18cm round cake. Just increase the cooking time to 35–40 minutes, or until the centre springs back to the touch.*

TRY THIS *For banana and cinnamon muffins, simply substitute a mashed medium-sized banana for the apple sauce.*

banana split muffins

This is a twist on an old favourite. It can be made lactose and dairy free by substituting in a dairy-free chocolate and using dairy-free baking spread in the topping. Melted coconut oil, blended along with the banana instead of the vegetable oil, is another delicious alternative.

175g GF Flour Mix A or GF
    Sorghum Flour Blend
    (page 15)
¼ level teaspoon xanthan gum
2 level teaspoons GF baking
    powder
3 medium eggs
125g soft dark brown sugar
2 teaspoons vanilla extract
1 small, very ripe banana
100ml vegetable oil
30g GF bitter dark chocolate,
    grated

FOR THE TOPPING
25g hazelnuts or almonds
200g soft salted butter or
    dairy-free margarine
150g icing sugar, sifted
75g dark GF chocolate, grated
1 small ripe banana, sliced
12 glacé or fresh cherries

Makes 8 large or 12 small · **PREP TIME** *10 minutes* · **COOKING TIME** *20 minutes*

1. Preheat the oven to 190°C/180°C fan/gas mark 5. Line a muffin tray with paper cases.

2. In a large bowl, sift the flour with the xanthan gum and baking powder.

3. Place the eggs, sugar and vanilla into a mixer or use an electric hand whisk and whisk for 2 minutes until thick.

4. Blend the banana with the oil until you have a thick purée. Stir this into the whisked egg mixture, then add the flour mixture and the grated chocolate. Stir well but don't beat; the mixture will be quite wet and should still look a little lumpy. Transfer the mixture to a jug.

5. Pour the batter evenly between the muffin cases. Bake in the middle of the oven for about 20 minutes, or until the surface springs back to the touch. Remove from the oven and leave to cool slightly in the tray before transferring to a wire rack to cool completely.

6. Heat a dry non-stick pan over a medium heat and toast the nuts for a few minutes until brown. Don't let them burn. Leave to cool and then chop.

7. In a bowl, whisk together the butter or spread and icing sugar until soft, light and creamy. Add the grated chocolate and mix well.

8. Fill a piping bag fitted with a star nozzle with the mixture and pipe swirls over each muffin, then decorate with the banana slices, chopped nuts and cherries.

classic vanilla sponge cake

This classic cake is really adaptable. You can tweak the sponge with different flavours like coffee and chocolate – see below for some suggestions. To make a classic Vanilla Sponge, just dust the top with a little caster sugar.

225g GF White and Brown Rice Flour Blend (page 15)

2 level teaspoons GF baking powder

1 level teaspoon xanthan gum

225g salted butter, at room temperature

225g caster sugar, plus extra to dust

4 medium eggs, at room temperature

1 teaspoon vanilla extract

3–4 tablespoons milk

6–8 tablespoons apricot jam or any fruit compote

FOR THE BUTTERCREAM ICING

175g unsalted butter, softened

350g icing sugar, sifted

½ teaspoon vanilla extract

2–3 teaspoons milk

Makes 1 x 20cm cake · **PREP TIME** *30 minutes* · **COOKING TIME** *25–30 minutes*

1. Preheat the oven to 190°C/180°C fan/gas mark 5. Line the bases of two 20cm spring-form cake tins with baking paper.

2. Sift the gluten-free flour, baking powder and xanthan gum into a bowl.

3. In a separate large bowl, beat together the butter and sugar for 2 minutes until light. Add the eggs, then fold in the flour mixture, beating until creamy. Stir in the vanilla extract and enough milk to make a soft mixture that drops from the spoon.

4. Divide the mixture evenly between the cake tins and level the surface. Bake on the same shelf in the centre of the oven for 25–30 minutes, until the sponge bounces back when touched. Leave to cool slightly, then turn out onto a wire rack to cool completely.

5. To make the icing, slowly beat together the butter and icing sugar until they start to come together, then increase the speed and beat for a few minutes until really light and fluffy. Add the vanilla and a little milk if the mixture is too stiff.

6. Place one of the sponges onto a plate and spread with the jam, then the buttercream icing. Top with the second sponge and dust the top with caster sugar. Set aside to give the icing time to set before serving.

VARIATIONS

COFFEE CAKE *Dissolve 1 tablespoon of instant coffee granules in 1 tablespoon of hot water and add to the mixture with the vanilla extract, instead of the milk. For the icing, instead of vanilla, flavour the buttercream with 1 teaspoon of coffee granules dissolved first in 1 teaspoon of hot water.*

CHOCOLATE SPONGE CAKE *Replace 25g of the flour blend with 25g of dark cocoa powder and add ½ teaspoon extra of xanthan gum. Grate 25g gluten-free dark chocolate into the flour mixture. Substitute light brown sugar for the caster sugar and ice the cake with Chocolate Truffle Ganache (page 237).*

tea loaf fruitcake

This is a perfect fruitcake for afternoon tea, or any other time, for that matter. You can use different spices and vary the selection of dried fruits. Jasmine tea is a good alternative to Earl Grey, too. This version is gluten, wheat and dairy free, but you can swap to butter and milk if you prefer. Speed is often the key to the success of gluten-free baking, but overbeating can make the batter sticky, so mix this cake gently using a hand-held electric whisk, and then fold in the fruit by hand.

450g mixed dried fruit or nuts (sultanas, raisins, apricots, dates, figs, glacé cherries)
75ml cold Earl Grey tea or brandy
175g GF Sorghum Flour Blend (page 15)
1½ teaspoons GF baking powder
1 level teaspoon xanthan gum
½ teaspoon GF mixed spice or ground cinnamon
90g dairy-free margarine
125g light soft brown sugar
2 teaspoons blackstrap molasses or treacle
2 medium eggs, beaten
100–125ml GF dairy-free milk

Serves 12 • **PREP TIME** *15 minutes, plus soaking* • **COOKING TIME** *1–1½ hours*

1. Place the dried fruit in a bowl, add the tea or brandy and stir well. Cover and leave until most of the liquid has been absorbed – overnight is ideal.

2. Preheat the oven to 160°C/150°C fan/gas mark 3. Line the base and sides of a 22 x 12cm loaf tin with a strip of baking parchment.

3. Sift the flour with the baking powder, xanthan gum and spice.

4. Place the margarine and sugar into a separate bowl and beat until creamy. Stir in the molasses or treacle. Add 2 tablespoons of flour to the mixture and combine.

5. Beat a little egg into the mixture, then some flour. Continue alternating until all the eggs and flour have been added. Stir in enough milk to give you a soft mixture that drops from the spoon. Don't overbeat. Finally, add the soaked fruit and fold through just until evenly mixed. Spoon into the prepared tin.

6. Bake for 1–1½ hours, until well risen and turning dark brown. The baking time will vary depending on your oven, but try not to open the oven door until the last few minutes, or the cake may sink. When it's ready, a skewer inserted into the centre of the cake should come out clean. Remove from the oven and cool in the tin for about 1 hour before turning out. When cold, wrap in greaseproof paper and then in foil. This cake keeps well and is even better after a day or two.

TIP *If you don't have time to soak the fruit for hours, boil it with half the tea or brandy for 2 minutes before adding the rest of the liquid. Leave to cool before using.*

TRY THIS *Make this as a tray bake and slice into individual bars. Bake in a 20cm square tray bake tin lined with baking paper. A smaller tin, or a small loaf tin is fine, but don't use a larger tin or the cake will be too thin. You could add a layer of gluten-free almond paste marzipan and icing before slicing.*

double chocolate almond cake

This is a simple cake with character; it will crackle and split on top as it rises and is more fluffy and close-textured than light and spongy. Rich and moist, it's gluten, wheat and dairy free. Serve a slice just as it is, or top with rich chocolate ganache.

175g GF White and Brown Rice Flour Blend (page 15)

2 teaspoons GF baking powder

½ level teaspoon xanthan gum

20g cocoa powder

200g dark soft brown sugar

50g ground almonds

20g GF dairy-free dark chocolate chips

3 medium eggs

100ml vegetable oil

100ml GF unsweetened almond milk

1 teaspoon vanilla extract or paste

1 quantity Chocolate Truffle Ganache (page 237) (optional)

a little GF grated chocolate, to sprinkle

Makes 1 x 18cm round cake • **PREP TIME** *15 minutes* • **COOKING TIME** *50–60 minutes*

1. Preheat the oven to 160°C/150°C fan/gas mark 3. Line the base of an 18cm spring-form cake tin with baking paper.

2. Sift the gluten-free flour into a bowl with the baking powder, xanthan gum and cocoa powder, and stir until evenly mixed. Stir in the sugar, breaking up any lumps. Add the ground almonds and stir in the chocolate chips.

3. In a separate large bowl, beat together the eggs, oil, milk and vanilla until combined. Fold the wet mixture into the dry ingredients and stir just until the batter is soft, loose and evenly mixed. Do not over-beat.

4. Spoon the mixture into the prepared tin so that it's level with the top and bake in the centre of the oven for about 1 hour until the surface has risen and springs back to the touch. A skewer inserted into the centre of the cake should come out clean or with a few crumbs, but not wet. Allow to cool, then turn the cake out onto a wire rack.

5. If you want to frost the cake with the chocolate truffle ganache, once it is completely cold, level the top if you need to, then slowly and carefully spread it over the top of the cake. Sprinkle with grated chocolate as it sets.

TRY THIS *Bake the mixture in a small loaf tin and cut into slices. Or make it into cupcakes and top with chocolate or vanilla buttercream (see page 227 for timings).*

NOTE *I used our gluten-free white and brown rice blend for this recipe, but remember, if you substitute a different blend the texture may change and you may need to adjust the liquid and xanthan gum accordingly. This cake will keep for a few days in an airtight container and freezes well.*

sweet potato tray bake squares with cinnamon buttercream

This is a great basic recipe, which you can tweak with other ingredients if you want to. Recipes containing puréed or grated vegetables like sweet potato, butternut squash, carrot, courgette and beetroot (or fruits) work well in gluten-free recipes; they help towards a moist texture and bind the crumb well. This recipe is also dairy free.

175g GF Sorghum Flour Blend (page 15)
2 teaspoons GF baking powder
¼ level teaspoon xanthan gum
1 level teaspoon GF mixed spice or ground cinnamon
120g light muscovado or soft brown sugar
100ml sunflower oil
3 medium eggs
175g sweet potato, cooked and puréed
1–2 tablespoons GF dairy-free milk

FOR THE BUTTERCREAM TOPPING
200g dairy-free cooking spread
450g icing sugar
1 teaspoon ground cinnamon
2 teaspoons boiled, cooled water

Makes 9 squares • **PREP TIME** *15 minutes* • **COOKING TIME** *30 minutes*

1. Preheat the oven to 180°C/170°C fan/gas mark 4. Line a 20cm square tin with baking paper.

2. Sift together the gluten-free flour, baking powder, xanthan gum and spice.

3. Place the sugar in a large bowl, and add the oil, whisking continuously using a hand-held electric whisk, then add the eggs, one at a time. Stir in the sweet potato, then fold in the flour mixture. Finally, add the milk to loosen and soften the mixture.

4. Spread the mixture into the prepared tin, level the top and bake in the middle of the oven for 25–30 minutes, until the cake springs back to the touch. Remove from the oven and cool for 5 minutes in the tin, then transfer to a wire rack to cool completely.

5. To make the buttercream, beat the margarine using an electric hand-held whisk until light and fluffy. In a separate bowl, sift the icing sugar and cinnamon together, and gradually beat this into the margarine, starting slowly and then increasing the speed. Add a little water until the mixture is smooth and creamy, but not too wet to pipe. Do not over-beat or the mixture may split.

6. Spread the buttercream in an even layer over the top of the cooled cake, then cut into squares. Alternatively, cut into squares first, then pipe a little swirl of buttercream on top. Keep the cakes chilled in the refrigerator after icing.

TIPS *To prepare the sweet potato, simply roast it in its skin until soft, then scrape out the flesh and mash.*

If using a spread or margarine for buttercream, make sure it's suitable for baking, and not low fat. Low-fat spreads contain too much water and the mixture can split. Some cooking margarines contain milk protein, so do check the product is dairy free.

little polenta cakes with passion fruit curd

This is a refreshing variation on a cupcake. You can make these cakes with any flavour of fruit curd, or top with a dollop of passion fruit cream. I like the texture of polenta, but you could make them with ground almonds instead. Watch out for the crunchy passion fruit seeds.

150g GF White and Brown Rice Flour Blend (page 15)

1 level teaspoon GF baking powder

¼ level teaspoon xanthan gum

25g very fine polenta, or ground almonds

150g unsalted butter, softened

150g caster sugar

3 medium eggs

110g buttermilk

FOR THE PASSION FRUIT CREAM

200g Passion Fruit Curd (page 238), well chilled, or 100g mascarpone or cream cheese

75g icing sugar, sifted

seeds and pulp of 2 small passion fruit

Makes 12 large cupcakes · **PREP TIME** *20 minutes* · **COOKING TIME** *25 minutes*

1. If you're not using curd, beat the mascarpone or cream cheese with the icing sugar and swirl the passion fruit pulp loosely through the mixture. Chill.

2. Preheat the oven to 190°C/180°C fan/gas mark 5. Line a 12-hole muffin tray with paper cases.

3. In a large bowl, sift the gluten-free flour with the gluten-free baking powder, xanthan gum and polenta.

4. In a separate bowl, cream the butter and sugar together until creamy and light. Add the eggs, beating in one at a time.

5. Add alternating spoonfuls of the buttermilk and flour, beating until evenly mixed and you have a soft cake batter. Spoon the mixture into the paper cases to about three-quarters full.

6. Bake in the centre of the oven for about 25 minutes until golden and the surface springs back to the touch. Transfer the cakes to a wire rack to cool.

7. Spoon a dollop of passion fruit curd or the mascarpone mixture onto each cake before serving.

lemon, lime & almond drizzle cake

This version of lemon drizzle is made with ground almonds and polenta flour to give it a fine texture to soak up the lemon syrup. Remember, the finer the ground polenta, the softer the end result will be. You can use any plain gluten-free flour.

115g GF flour, such as GF
 Polenta Flour Blend
 (page 14)
¼ level teaspoon xanthan gum
1 level teaspoon GF baking
 powder
150g caster sugar
50g finely ground almonds
2 medium eggs
175g dairy-free margarine,
 melted
finely grated zest of 1 large
 unwaxed lemon
finely grated zest and juice
 of 1 large unwaxed lime
juice of 1 large lemon
25g granulated sugar

Serves 12 · **PREP TIME** *15 minutes* · **COOKING TIME** *40–50 minutes*

1. Preheat the oven to 190°C/180°C fan/gas mark 5. Line a 20cm square tin with baking paper.

2. In a large bowl, sift the flour with the xanthan gum and baking powder. Stir in the caster sugar and the ground almonds.

3. In a small bowl, mix together the eggs, melted margarine, lemon and lime zests and the lime juice. Pour the wet mixture into the dry ingredients and use an electric hand mixer, starting at a low speed, then increasing to high, to beat the mixture until smooth, like a batter. Pour into the tin and tap it lightly on the work surface to remove any air pockets.

4. Bake in the middle of the oven for 40–50 minutes, until the surface is springy to the touch. Remove from the oven and leave in its tin.

5. Mix the lemon juice with the granulated sugar and, while the cake is still warm in its tin, spoon the lemon and sugar mixture over the surface.

6. Allow to cool completely then cut into slices. This cake will keep for a few days in an airtight container, and freezes well.

TIP *If you don't have a 20cm tray bake tin, use a smaller tin, or even a small loaf tin, but don't use anything larger or the cake will be too thin.*

TRY THIS *This cake is delicious as it is, but you can dress it up with a simple glaze icing. Sift 125g of icing sugar into a large bowl. Gradually add 1–2 teaspoons of boiled, cooled water (or lemon or lime juice), beating well after each addition. If necessary, add extra water until the icing is smooth, soft and easy to spread. It should be firm enough to stay in place but not solid. Drizzle over the cooled cake and leave to set.*

madeleines

Madeleines are elegant little cakes that are just lovely served with coffee. These ones are made in the traditional French way: golden, with deliciously crisp edges and a little hump. For good texture, they are best cooked in a conventional oven rather than a fan oven. It also helps if you chill the batter just before baking so that it thickens up enough to spoon into the moulds more easily.

100g GF White and Brown Rice Flour Blend (pages 15), plus extra for dusting
½ level teaspoon GF baking powder
2 medium eggs, at room temperature
a pinch of salt
1 teaspoon vanilla extract
75g caster sugar
1 teaspoon grated lemon zest
75g unsalted butter, melted and cooled, plus extra for greasing

Makes 24 · **PREP TIME** *15 minutes, plus 20 minutes chilling* · **COOKING TIME** *10 minutes*

1. Preheat the oven to 220°C/gas mark 7. Grease a 12-hole madeleine tray or cupcake tray with butter, then dust with gluten-free flour and tap out the excess.

2. Sift together the gluten-free flour and baking powder and set aside.

3. Put the eggs in a mixer with the salt and beat for 3–4 minutes until thick and doubled volume. Add the vanilla and the sugar in a slow trickle, continuing to beat for another 5 minutes until the mixture is thick and leaves a ribbon trail.

4. Sprinkle the lemon zest over the whipped mixture and sift over the flour. Fold in very gently. Trickle the cooled, melted butter at the edge of the mixture and fold this in very carefully until evenly combined. Chill the mixture in the fridge for 15–20 minutes.

5. Spoon half the mixture into the moulds so that each hole is three-quarters full (one-third if you are using a cupcake tray). Refrigerate the rest of the batter. Bake for 8–10 minutes until dark golden, well risen and hopefully with a little hump in the middle of each cake. Tip the madeleines out of the tray straight away and cool on a wire rack. Grease and dust the moulds again, and cook the second batch.

TRY THIS *Dip one half of the madeleines in gluten-free melted chocolate and leave to set.*

chocolate fairy cakes

These delicious cakes are egg, gluten and dairy free. The wet and dry ingredients need to be combined quickly because as soon as the acidity of the lemon juice meets the baking powder, bubbles will start to form and these are essential for ending up with light and airy cakes.

200ml GF soya or almond milk

60ml vegetable oil

1 teaspoon vanilla extract

2 teaspoons lemon juice or cider vinegar

100g caster sugar

200g GF White and Brown Rice Flour Blend (page 15)

1½ teaspoons GF baking powder

¼ level teaspoon xanthan gum

4 tablespoons cocoa powder

25g GF dairy-free chocolate chips (optional)

FOR THE CHOCOLATE GLACÉ

100g icing sugar

1 tablespoon cocoa powder

about 1–2 teaspoons boiled, cooled water

grated GF dairy-free chocolate, GF sprinkles or glacé cherries, to decorate

Makes 12 · **PREP TIME** *10 minutes chilling* · **COOKING TIME** *15 minutes*

1. Preheat the oven to 160°C/160°C fan/gas mark 3 and line a 12-hole cupcake tray with paper cases.

2. In a bowl, mix together the milk, oil, vanilla extract and lemon juice or vinegar. It won't fully blend, but that is okay.

3. In a separate bowl, stir together the sugar, flour, baking powder, xanthan gum and cocoa powder, then add the chocolate chips, if using.

4. Quickly pour the liquid mixture into the dry ingredients and stir to combine, then evenly divide the cake mixture between the paper cases. Bake for about 15 minutes until firm, then cool on a wire rack.

5. To make the glaze, sieve the icing sugar and cocoa powder into a large bowl. Gradually add the water, beating well after each addition, until you have a paste. If necessary, add extra water until the icing is smooth, soft and easy to spread. It should be firm enough to stay in place but not solid.

6. Spread the glacé over the cakes with a metal spoon. Top with grated chocolate, sprinkles or a glacé cherry before the icing sets.

sweet ricotta doughnuts

These are fabulous little morsels; just make sure the oil is hot enough and the inside will be fluffy and light. The recipe makes about 30 doughnuts, to allow four servings of six little bites. Double up if you need to make more.

vegetable oil, for deep-
  frying (see note about
  contamination on page 8)
1 egg, beaten
1 egg yolk
45g GF White and Brown Rice
  Flour Blend (page 15)
1 teaspoon caster sugar
1 level teaspoon GF baking
  powder
1/8 level teaspoon xanthan gum
finely grated zest of 1 lemon
250g ricotta cheese, drained
  overnight
fine sugar or icing sugar,
  to dust
a pinch of ground cinnamon,
  to dust (optional)

Makes about 30 · **PREP TIME** *10 minutes* · **COOKING TIME** *25 minutes*

1. Heat the oil to 180°C in a deep-fat fryer or deep-sided pan filled one-third with oil.

2. Place the egg and yolk in a bowl, add the flour, sugar, baking powder, xanthan gum and lemon zest, and mix really well. Add the ricotta and mix again.

3. Using a piping bag (not fitted with a nozzle) pipe small balls of the mixture straight into the hot oil. Cook a small batch at a time until nice and golden, for about 3 minutes, turning the doughnuts to get an even colour. If you don't have a piping bag, roll balls of batter between metal spoons and transfer to the oil with a slotted spoon.

4. Drain well on kitchen paper and sprinkle with fine sugar or icing sugar and cinnamon, if you like. Serve straight away.

TRY THIS *If you pipe the dough in a straight line using a large star nozzle, the result will be like Spanish churros. Sprinkle with sugar and serve with a gluten-free chocolate dip.*

classic vanilla cupcakes

Here is an updated cupcake recipe that can be made with either soft butter or margarine. They can be topped with a variety of toppings and creams – see pages 236–239 for inspiration.

175g GF White and Brown Rice Flour Blend (page 15)
175g unsalted butter, at room temperature
175g caster sugar
3 medium eggs, at room temperature
1 level teaspoon GF baking powder
¾ level teaspoon xanthan gum
½ teaspoon vanilla extract

FOR THE ICING
175g soft unsalted butter or margarine
350g icing sugar, sifted
½ teaspoon vanilla extract
2–3 teaspoons milk
edible food colouring
GF edible sprinkles, to decorate

Makes 12 • **PREP TIME** *15 minutes* • **COOKING TIME** *20–25 minutes*

1. Preheat the oven to 190°C/180°C fan/gas mark 5. Line a 12-hole cupcake tray with paper cases.

2. Put all the cake ingredients into a large bowl and beat with an electric hand whisk until smooth and evenly mixed. Divide the mixture evenly between the paper cases.

3. Bake for 20–25 minutes, or until the cakes are well risen and firm on top. Transfer to a wire rack to cool.

4. In a bowl, slowly beat the butter or margarine for the icing with the sifted icing sugar until it starts to come together, then increase the speed and beat for a few minutes until really light and fluffy.

5. Add the vanilla and a little milk, if needed, to loosen the consistency.

6. Now you can colour the icing: dip a cocktail stick into your food colouring of choice and mix it into the icing in small drops until you like the colour.

7. Spread the icing over the cupcakes and have fun with a few gluten-free sprinkles on top. Eat fresh or freeze (with or without the icing).

TRY THIS *Stir 50g of chopped walnuts through the cake batter before you fill the cupcake cases and flavour the buttercream with 1 teaspoon of coffee granules dissolved in 1 teaspoon of hot water instead of the milk.*

TIP *Gluten-free cupcakes are best eaten fresh, or they can be frozen. I find that foil cupcake cases are less likely to peel away and separate from the sides once the cupcakes have defrosted.*

carrot cupcakes with cream cheese frosting

Carrot cake is always popular; if you'd rather make a small loaf cake instead of cupcakes, just cook it a little longer than recommended here. Make the frosting before baking the cakes to give it time to chill – it's too soft to use straight away. You can add a touch of cinnamon, orange zest or chopped stem ginger, if you like.

1 quantity Cream Cheese Icing
  (page 237)
175g GF Sorghum Flour Blend
  (page 15)
¼ level teaspoon xanthan gum
2 teaspoons GF baking powder
½ teaspoon bicarbonate
  of soda
1 level teaspoon GF mixed
  spice or ground cinnamon
120g light muscovado or soft
  brown sugar
100ml sunflower oil
3 medium eggs, at room
  temperature
175g carrots, peeled, coarsely
  grated and squeezed dry
1–2 tablespoons milk
GF sprinkles, to decorate

Makes 12 · **PREP TIME** *15 minutes* · **COOKING TIME** *30 minutes*

1. Preheat the oven to 190°C/180°C fan/gas mark 5. Line a 12-hole muffin tin with large cupcake cases.

2. First make the cream cheese icing, then chill.

3. In a bowl, sift together the gluten-free flour, xanthan gum, gluten-free baking powder, bicarbonate of soda and spice.

4. Place the sugar into a separate large bowl. Add the oil and the eggs, one at a time, whisking continuously with a hand-held electric whisk. Stir in the carrots then fold in the sifted dry ingredients. Add the milk to loosen and soften the mixture.

5. Divide the batter between the cases so that they are about three-quarters full. Bake in the centre of the oven for 25–30 minutes. The cakes are done when the centre springs back when lightly pressed. Remove from the oven and transfer to a wire rack to cool completely.

6. To decorate the cupcakes, fill a disposable piping bag fitted with a large star nozzle with the icing. Start at the outside edge, piping round the edge of the cake in a spiral towards the centre. Pull up quickly to finish the swirl. Finish with some sprinkles. Keep the cakes chilled in the refrigerator after icing.

chocolate brownies with peanut buttercream & chocolate truffle icing

Dark, rich and divine – these brownies make irresistible treats. The chopped chocolate melts into the fudgy sponge and a double topping of peanut buttercream and chocolate truffle ganache is the icing on the cake. They're more of a dessert than a cake but you can, of course, leave the brownies unadorned. The brownie will probably crack on top as it bakes and then sink down after you take it out of the oven. Slightly under baking is essential for that quintessential fudgy brownie texture; a bit too long in the oven and you will end up with cake.

125g unsalted butter

150g GF dark chocolate

175g dark brown soft sugar

2 large eggs

1 teaspoon vanilla extract

55g GF White and Brown Rice Flour Blend (page 15)

1 level teaspoon GF baking powder

1 quantity Peanut Buttercream (page 236)

1 quantity Chocolate Truffle Ganache (page 237)

Makes 12 · **PREP TIME** *40 minutes, plus 1 hour chilling* · **COOKING TIME** *30 minutes*

1. Preheat the oven to 180°C/170°C fan/gas mark 4. Line an 18cm square tin with baking paper.

2. In a small pan, melt the butter with 50g of the chocolate, then set aside to cool. Chop the remaining 100g of chocolate into rough chunks.

3. In a large bowl beat together the sugar with the eggs and vanilla. Sift the flour with the baking powder and mix this into the eggs and sugar. Stir in the cooled, melted chocolate mixture, add the chocolate chunks and mix until combined, then pour the mixture into the tin.

4. Bake for about 30 minutes, until the brownie begins to shrink from the sides of the tin and has a crust on top. It should still be soft and a little wobbly in the centre. Take it out of the oven and leave it to cool in the tin. If you're not adding the toppings, cut into squares and serve. If you are, chill it in the fridge.

5. Once the brownie is cold, top with a thin layer of the smooth peanut buttercream, return to the fridge to chill, then pour a thin layer of chocolate truffle ganache over the top. Return to the fridge to set, then cut into squares. Eat at room temperature.

simple chocolate glacé icing

125g icing sugar
25g cocoa powder
1–2 teaspoons boiled, cooled
   water

Makes enough for a small cake or 12 cupcakes • **PREP TIME** *10 minutes*

Sift the icing sugar with the cocoa powder into a large bowl. Gradually add the boiled, cooled water, beating well after each addition. If necessary, add extra water until the icing is smooth, soft and easy to spread. It should be firm enough to stay in place but not solid.

vanilla buttercream

175g unsalted butter, softened
½ teaspoon vanilla bean paste
   or 1 teaspoon vanilla extract
2–3 tablespoons milk
300g icing sugar, sifted

Makes enough for 12 cupcakes • **PREP TIME** *10 minutes*

Put the butter, vanilla, 2 tablespoons of the milk and half the icing sugar into a large bowl, and beat until smooth. Beat in the remaining icing sugar and the rest of the milk, if needed, to make the icing the right consistency. Whisk until light and fluffy.

STRAWBERRY OR BERRY *Add 1 tablespoon of jam strained through a sieve.*
COFFEE AND WALNUT *Add 1 teaspoon of instant coffee granules dissolved in 2 teaspoons of hot water. Top the frosting with chopped or crushed walnuts.*
PASSION FRUIT *Swirl in the pulp from 1 small passion fruit.*
CITRUS *Add 1 tablespoon of finely grated zest from 1 unwaxed lemon or lime, and 2 teaspoons of juice.*

peanut buttercream

55g unsalted butter, softened
125g smooth GF peanut butter,
   at room temperature
125g icing sugar
2 tablespoons GF coconut milk
   or any other milk

Makes enough for 18cm cake or 6 cupcakes • **PREP TIME** *10 minutes*

Put the butter and peanut butter into a bowl and beat with an electric mixer. Gradually mix in the icing sugar, and when it starts to thicken, incorporate the coconut milk, 1 tablespoon at a time, until all the sugar is mixed in, and the icing is thick and spreadable. Beat for about 3 minutes until fluffy.

chocolate buttercream

125g unsalted butter, softened
200g icing sugar, sifted
50g cocoa powder, sifted
1 teaspoon vanilla extract
   or water

Makes enough to fill and top a 20cm round cake • **PREP TIME** *10 minutes*

Beat the butter with the icing sugar, cocoa powder and vanilla or enough water until you have a soft cream.

chocolate truffle ganache

To make a dairy-free ganache, substitute in 200ml almond or other dairy-free milk and 300g dairy-free chocolate.

125g GF dark chocolate,
   chopped
a small knob of butter
150ml whipping cream

Makes enough to top an 18cm round cake • **PREP TIME** *10 minutes, plus cooling*

Melt the chocolate with the butter and cream in a heavy-based pan over a low heat. Stir and make sure the mixture doesn't get too hot – you don't want it to boil. Just before the chocolate has finished melting, take it off the heat and stir until smooth, thick and glossy. Pour into a bowl to cool.

cream cheese icing

Make this icing before you bake your cake as it's too soft to use straight away and will need time to chill and set. Don't over-beat a cream cheese frosting as it is liable to curdle. Use full-fat soft cheese and drain it well: low-fat versions tend to thin or separate after beating.

150g full-fat cream cheese,
   drained
300g icing sugar, sifted
75g unsalted butter, softened
½ tsp vanilla essence

Makes enough to top 12 cupcakes • **PREP TIME** *10 minutes*

In a bowl, beat together half the cream cheese with half the icing sugar and all the butter. Add the remaining cream cheese and icing sugar along with the vanilla, and whisk until light and fluffy. Add a little water, if needed.

cream cheese icing made with dates

This recipe makes a sweet, lower-sugar filling or topping for cakes. Medjool dates add a caramel flavour.

50g soft medjool dates, finely
chopped, or dried dates
soaked in 50ml boiling water
for 10 minutes
125g full-fat cream cheese,
drained

Makes 200g · **PREP TIME** *10 minutes*

1. Blend the dates until smooth and then chill.

2. Whip the cream cheese with a hand-held electric whisk, then slowly add the date purée, whipping until you have a light, creamy spread. Chill before using.

passion fruit curd

Passion fruit makes a change from lemon or lime curds. Just make sure you press as much purée and juice form the fruits as possible. Try not to turn the heat up to speed things up – if the pan is too hot, the eggs will scramble and catch on the bottom, so cook gently.

pulp, seeds and juice of 8 ripe
passion fruit
4 medium eggs
150g caster sugar
100g unsalted butter, melted
and cooled

Makes about 350ml · **PREP TIME** *15 minutes* · **COOKING TIME** *10 minutes*

1. Put the pulp, seeds and juice of 7 of the passion fruit into a food-processor or use a stick blender. Blitz to loosen the seeds, then strain into a bowl, pushing through as much pulp as you can. Discard the dry seeds.

2. Beat together the eggs and sugar until just frothy. Stir the mixture into the cooled butter along with the strained passion fruit juice. Pour into a pan over a low heat and stir constantly until the mixture has thickened to the consistency of a loose lemon curd. This can take up to 10 minutes.

3. Take the pan off the heat, stir in the pulp and seeds of the reserved passion fruit. Pour the curd into sterilised jars, cool and keep in the fridge for up to one week.

dairy-free vanilla icing

The water content of dairy-free margarine varies: check whether it is suitable for baking and is not a low-fat soft spread. Only beat for a couple of minutes as it can easily be overwhipped and split.

125g dairy-free baking margarine
250g icing sugar, sifted
½ teaspoon vanilla bean paste or 1 teaspoon vanilla extract
1 teaspoon boiled, cooled water

Makes enough to fill a 20cm cake • **PREP TIME** *10 minutes*

Beat the margarine and half the icing sugar together. Add the remaining sugar and the vanilla, then whisk until light and fluffy. Add a drop of water if needed until you have a smooth and creamy buttercream consistency.

dairy-free chocolate icing

Double the recipe for frosting on top as well as filling, or for cupcakes.

100g dairy-free baking margarine, softened
40g cocoa powder, sifted
300g icing sugar, sifted

Makes enough for 12 cupcakes • **PREP TIME** *10 minutes*

Whip together the margarine, cocoa powder and icing sugar until the mixture comes together and is well mixed. Add 1 or 2 tablespoons of cold water to the mixture to get the right consistency.

dairy-free chocolate buttercream filling

You can replace half the margarine with coconut oil for a subtle coconut flavour.

100g GF dairy-free chocolate, chopped
100g dairy-free baking margarine, softened
100g icing sugar

Makes enough to fill 1 x 20cm cake • **PREP TIME** *10 minutes, plus cooling*

1. Melt the chocolate in a large bowl set over a pan of hot, but not boiling, water. Make sure the base of the bowl doesn't touch the water.

2. Remove from the heat and add the margarine, stirring to melt. Add the icing sugar and beat until you have a fluffy buttercream.

spices, sauces & stuffings

toasted coconut & coriander chutney

In the Oberoi Hotel in Delhi I had something very similar to this for lunch one day to accompany tandoori prawns. It was served with the lightest naan bread I have ever eaten; I will never forget it.

150g desiccated coconut
150g fresh coriander, including
   stalks, washed
5 garlic cloves, roughly
   chopped
1 tablespoon caster or
   granulated sugar
juice of 2 large limes
2 tablespoons chopped
   fresh red chilli
2 tablespoons vegetable oil
salt

Serves 4 • **PREP TIME** *15 minutes* • **COOKING TIME** *5 minutes*

1. Place the desiccated coconut in a shallow pan over a medium heat and toast gently until golden brown.

2. Place the toasted coconut, coriander, garlic, sugar, lime juice, chilli and oil into a food-processor and blitz until you have a thick purée. You may need to add a little cold water if it's too thick. Spoon into a bowl and season with salt. Store in an airtight jar and refrigerate for up to two weeks.

green chilli dressing

2 tablespoons finely sliced
   ginger or galangal
3 large garlic cloves, crushed
1 jalapeño chilli, finely
   chopped
4 tablespoons roughly
   chopped fresh coriander
4 tablespoons chopped Thai
   or regular basil
salt
a pinch of sugar
juice and finely grated zest
   of 4 limes

A delicious dressing for lettuce or any green-leaf vegetable such as spinach, Chinese leaves or finely sliced cabbage. I sometimes stir it through warm roasted vegetables, raw finely sliced fennel and celeriac, or even boiled new potatoes.

Serves 4 • **PREP TIME** *10 minutes*

Place the ginger or galangal, garlic, chilli and herbs into a bowl and mix really well. Season with salt, sugar and the lime zest and juice, and mix well. Leave to marinate for 15 minutes before serving.

ras el hanout sprinkle

4 tablespoons cumin seeds
3 teaspoons whole black peppercorns
8 black or green cardamom pods, crushed
2 teaspoons ground turmeric
1 tablespoon ground cinnamon
1 teaspoon ground ginger

A warm, fragrant North African spice mix, perfect for sprinkling over gluten-free crispy fried noodles or adding to stews and lamb tagines.

Serves 4 • **PREP TIME** *5 minutes* • **COOKING TIME** *2–3 minutes*

Heat a small non-stick frying pan over a low heat and gently toast all the spices, making sure they don't burn. This will take a couple of minutes. Cool, then either pound in a pestle and mortar or blitz in a food-processor. Store in an airtight jar.

Cajun spice sprinkle

1 tablespoon smoked paprika
1 tablespoon ground garlic
1 tablespoon dried oregano
1 tablespoon soft brown sugar
3 teaspoons salt
2 teaspoons ground black pepper
2 teaspoons dried thyme
1 teaspoon cayenne powder
½ teaspoon dried chilli flakes
½ teaspoon dried cumin

This is a really powerful spice mix that's great sprinkled over crispy gluten-free noodles or popcorn.

Serves 4 • **PREP TIME** *10 minutes*

Mix all the ingredients together really well and sprinkle away. Store in an airtight jar.

baharat spice sprinkle

1 tablespoon whole black peppercorns
2 tablespoons coriander seeds
6 cardamom pods, crushed
3 tablespoons cumin seeds
1 tablespoon ground cloves
1 tablespoon paprika
1 tablespoon smoked paprika
2 teaspoons grated nutmeg
1 teaspoon salt

I use two varieties of paprika to give a smoky flavour, but unsmoked will work just as well. Sprinkle over popcorn, meats or fish before grilling, or use as a seasoning for vegetables and rice.

Serves 4 • **PREP TIME** *5 minutes* • **COOKING TIME** *1–2 minutes*

Heat a non-stick frying pan over a low heat. Add the peppercorns, coriander seeds, cardamom and cumin, and toast gently for 1–2 minutes. Cool, then either pound in a pestle and mortar or blitz in a food-processor. Stir in the cloves, paprika, nutmeg and salt. Store in an airtight jar.

TIP *Coffee grinders are great for grinding spices, but use a separate one for your coffee or you'll get some unwelcome flavours in your morning cuppa.*

easy spiced plum sauce

4 tablespoons vegetable oil

1 small onion, finely diced

2 garlic cloves, peeled

1 tablespoon finely chopped
  ginger

2 tablespoons ground
  cinnamon

350g Victoria plums, stoned
  and roughly chopped

50g light brown sugar

3 tablespoons sherry vinegar

1 x 10g GF vegetable stock
  cube

salt and ground black pepper

This sauce is great with roast duck or pork and crackling.
It also makes a good sauce for stir-fries.

Serves 4–6 • **PREP TIME** *15 minutes* • **COOKING TIME** *20 minutes*

Heat the oil in a pan over a low heat and cook the onion, garlic, ginger and cinnamon for 5 minutes. Add the plums, sugar, vinegar, stock cube, along with of 300ml water. Season with salt and pepper and cook for 20 minutes, or until the plums are soft and pulpy. Blend until smooth, check the seasoning and serve warm.

apricot, celery & wholegrain mustard stuffing

25g butter

125g celery, finely chopped

1 red onion, finely chopped

1 egg, beaten

125g dried apricots, finely
  chopped

100g fresh white GF
  breadcrumbs

1–2 tablespoons fresh sage
  or flat-leaf parsley, finely
  chopped

1 teaspoon GF Dijon mustard

zest of 1 lemon

freshly grated nutmeg

salt and ground black pepper

This fruity stuffing is delicious with a roast and also for stuffing peppers or courgettes. It makes a delicious accompaniment to fish and chicken, too.

Serves 4 • **PREP TIME** *10 minutes* • **COOKING TIME** *10 minutes*

Melt the butter in a pan over a low heat and cook the celery and onion for 5–10 minutes until softened. Tip into a bowl, cool, then add the remaining ingredients. Mix well to bind.

TRY THIS

Use the stuffing to fill peppers, etc. before finishing in the oven.

For a side dish, tip into a greased ovenproof dish and cook at 180°C/gas mark 4 for 5–10 minutes until the egg is cooked through.

Serve as a light vegetarian dish, or with a fillet of fish, like salmon, by mixing with 250g of cooked mixed grains, such as brown basmati rice and quinoa that's been cooked in gluten-free stock.

pork & apple stuffing

Sausage meat stuffing with sweet fruit is a good partner for roast meats and poultry. You can easily vary the herbs and swap the apple with semi-dried apricots.

1 tablespoon vegetable oil

1 medium onion, chopped

2 crisp green apples, or 50g semi-dried apricots, finely chopped

500g GF sausage meat, chopped

1 garlic clove, crushed

100g GF breadcrumbs

1–2 tablespoons fresh thyme, chopped

1 egg, beaten

salt and ground black pepper

Serves 8 • **PREP TIME** *15 minutes* • **COOKING TIME** *15 minutes*

1. Preheat the oven to 180°C/gas mark 4. Grease an ovenproof dish.

2. Heat the oil in a pan over a low heat and cook the onion and apples for 5–10 minutes until soft and golden. If you are using apricots instead of apples, skip this step.

3. Add the sausage meat and garlic and cook for about 5 minutes, stirring, until browned on the outside. Remove from the heat, cool slightly and add the breadcrumbs, herbs, the beaten egg and seasoning. If you're using apricots, add them now. Mix everything well.

4. Tip the stuffing into the prepared dish and cook for about 15 minutes.

TRY THIS *Make sage and onion stuffing by replacing the thyme with sage, using 2 onions and leaving out the fruit.*

cranberry & cashew nut stuffing

See the tips above for how to use this stuffing as a delicious base for a main dish or a vegetarian option.

25g butter

2 medium onions, chopped

4 tablespoons chopped parsley

75g cashew nuts, toasted and chopped

50g dried cranberries

100g fresh white GF breadcrumbs

salt and ground black pepper

a pinch of grated nutmeg

zest of 1 lemon, plus 1 tablespoons of juice

1 egg, beaten

Serves 4 • **PREP TIME** *15 minutes* • **COOKING TIME** *15 minutes*

Melt the butter in a pan over a low heat and cook the onions for 5–10 minutes until soft and golden. Tip into a bowl and mix in the parsley, cashew nuts, cranberries and breadcrumbs. Season with salt and pepper, nutmeg and the lemon zest and juice, and leave to cool. Add the beaten egg and mix well to bind.

fruity fragrant stuffing

This is a great stuffing for the Christmas roast. I sometimes just make some up and eat it with a soft-boiled egg or some sautéed smoked gluten-free tofu.

6 tablespoons vegetable oil
1 tablespoon garam masala
½ teaspoon ground cardamom
½ teaspoon ground allspice
½ teaspoon smoked paprika
2 red onions, finely chopped
3 garlic cloves, finely chopped
2 tablespoons finely chopped ginger
100g dried apricots, finely chopped
100g dried cranberries, finely chopped
100g dried cherries, finely chopped
500g cooked coconut rice, hot
100g pistachios, roughly chopped
50g GF honey-roasted cashews, roughly chopped
salt and ground black pepper
1 egg, beaten (optional)
6 tablespoons chopped fresh parsley
2 tablespoons chopped fresh sage

Serves 6–8 • **PREP TIME** *20 minutes* • **COOKING TIME** *15 minutes*

1. Preheat the oven to 190°C/180°C fan/gas mark 5. Grease an ovenproof dish.

2. Heat the oil in a pan and quickly fry the spices. Lower the heat and add the onions, garlic and ginger. Cook for 10 minutes to soften nicely.

3. Spoon the mixture into a bowl and add the dried fruit, hot rice and nuts. Mix really well. Season well with salt and pepper.

4. Finally, add the egg to bind, if using, and the parsley and sage. Mix well. Use to stuff the bird or tip into a lightly greased baking dish and bake separately for about 15 minutes.

simple butter sauce (beurre blanc)

French beurre blanc is one of my favourite sauces as it's pretty much perfect with any meat or vegetable dish. The secret is to reduce the vinegar enough so that the butter emulsifies the sauce.

2 tablespoons white wine
   vinegar
100ml dry white wine
2 shallots, very finely chopped
a pinch of salt
a pinch of ground black pepper
6 tablespoons whipping cream
55–75g cold butter, cut into
   small cubes
1 small bunch of chives,
   very finely chopped

Serves 4 • **PREP TIME** *5 minutes* • **COOKING TIME** *15 minutes*

1. Put the vinegar, wine, shallots, salt and pepper into a pan and bring to the boil. Cook down until you are left with about 2–3 tablespoons of liquid. Add the cream to the pan, stir and bring back to the boil. Cook until the sauce starts to thicken.

2. Remove the pan from the heat and gradually add the cubes of butter, whisking all the time. The sauce will thicken naturally. If the butter does not melt from the residual heat return the pan to a very low heat just to warm through, but do not boil.

3. Take the pan off the heat and check the seasoning and adjust if needed. Keep the sauce warm and covered until serving, then add the chives at the last minute so that they keep their colour.

white sauce

A basic white sauce is useful for many dishes, such as moussaka. You can add a little more butter or margarine for a creamier sauce.

500ml milk
35g cornflour
35g butter, softened
a pinch of grated nutmeg
   (optional)
ground black pepper

Makes about 500ml • **PREP TIME** *10 minutes* • **COOKING TIME** *5 minutes*

1. Heat the milk to a simmer in a pan over a medium heat.

2. Meanwhile, in a small bowl, work the cornflour and butter together to make a paste.

3. Break off small pieces of the paste and whisk it into the simmering milk. The sauce will thicken almost immediately. Add the nutmeg, if using, and pepper, then remove from the heat but keep warm. Place a layer of cling film over the surface to prevent a skin forming before serving.

AMARANTH

Amaranth flour is ground from a small seed, high in protein and rich in iron. A small amount of the flour can be mixed into your gluten-free flour blend. Like many seeds, it has an assertive taste.

ARROWROOT

A very fine white starch; lightens the crumb in baking and will hold a nice structure to sponges and flour-based products. For thickening and binding, it will set clearer than cornflour. Arrowroot can be substituted for potato starch and cornflour in recipes, but is more expensive.

BAKING POWDER

Helps to give a light and airy texture to baked products. Its raising properties come from a mixture of an alkali (bicarbonate of soda) and an acid (cream of tartar). When the dry powder is mixed with water, bubbles of carbon dioxide are produced and expand during baking, to provide the aeration to sponges, pastries and biscuits. Make sure you check the label as some baking powders are not gluten free: wheat is added to absorb moisture in the powder.

When used in a creamed margarine-based sponge it will give a very light end result. Once your mixture is 'wet', the powder is activated, so don't leave it standing long before baking.

BROWN AND WHITE RICE FLOURS

Brown and white rice flours have a slightly gritty texture and are ideally combined with other flours for cooking, to lessen this sandy texture. Good for all-purpose, light and mild-flavoured baked goods.

Brown rice flour is ground from the whole rice kernel with some of the bran so it has more protein, fibre and is a little darker in colour and richer in flavour than white rice.

Sorghum flour can be used in preference to brown rice flour for a finer texture (see Sorghum p252).

BUCKWHEAT FLOUR

Buckwheat is a fruit seed. The plant is related to rhubarb, sorrel and dock, and is an excellent source of magnesium, zinc and iron. The flour has a slightly earthy flavour, and blended with other flour combinations, makes wonderful pancakes and noodles. Use the flakes in crumbles, granola, etc. The nibs make a good alternative to couscous.

Although buckwheat is naturally gluten free, check the source for possible contamination: unless guaranteed, it can have traces from the processing or from wheat handled nearby.

CHESTNUT FLOUR

Chestnut flour can be added in small amounts to other flours to give a delicate softness and sweet character to the end result. You can use a proportion of chestnut flour in place of sorghum or brown rice flour. It is high in starch, lower in fat and calories than other 'nut' flours and high in protein. Best to keep it in the fridge as it goes stale fairly quickly.

COCONUT FLOUR

A heavier, denser flour that will soak up more liquid than regular flours: be careful of using too much of it in recipes. The milk, cream and oil from coconut are versatile in a huge range of recipes (especially dairy-free) and impart a subtle coconut flavour.

COCONUT OIL

Coconut oil is extracted from coconut flesh and is solid at room temperature. It makes a useful dairy-free substitute for butter in icings and cakes. The oil is solid at room temperature, melts easily and is very stable for frying, roasting or baking.

Coconut oil is as high in calories as any other fat and includes saturated fat; but debate seems to err on the side of it being a good type of fat to use. Read labels carefully and choose raw or unrefined: cheaper coconut oil is hydrogenated.

CHIA SEEDS

Chia seeds have natural gelling properties that make them a good substitute for xanthan gum in recipes. Soaking in water enhances the gelling, but they remain as seeds. Tiny but mighty chia seeds are a rich source of fibre, protein and omega-3.

COOKING MARGARINE

A combination of oils, fats and sometimes milk proteins emulsified together. If you are looking for a substitute for butter or to use less saturated fat, make sure the baking spread you choose has a low water content and is suitable for baking and cooking. Some vegetable spreads have a high water content and will split easily on heating. Vegetable oil is an excellent substitute for solid fat in gluten-free cooking, although you will have to use it differently.

CORNFLOUR

Cornflour is milled from maize into a fine white powder with a bland taste that makes it ideal for baking. Not the same as golden coloured maize flour, which has a heavier structure. Cornflour needs to be added to other flours to get an optimum overall texture. Useful for thickening and as part of a blend of gluten-free flour, cornflour is used to lighten the crumb and helps with crispness in baking: great for biscuits, cookies and shortbread.

CORNMEAL OR FINE POLENTA

Polenta is essentially the same thing as cornmeal and made from dried, ground maize (corn). You will find a confusing variety of textures suitable for different dishes. Polenta is a useful source of fibre, a good source of zinc, B vitamins, magnesium and iron. It can add body and texture to bread, muffins or stuffing, or lend a mild, sweet flavour and a yellow colour.

Quick-cook polenta tends to have large grains and is pre-cooked to make a thick purée. For cakes, a fine-ground polenta meal is what you are looking for instead. Maize flour is golden and more powdery than polenta, but it is still a heavier texture than cornstarch or cornflour, which is also processed from maize.

Masa harina is a type of cornmeal used to make tortillas (page 34). The cornmeal is modified so that the proteins will form the characteristic dough.

FLAXSEED

Flaxseeds and linseeds (same thing) are little gems for nutrient value as well as having binding properties: in liquid they form a gel that can act as a useful substitute for eggs. Added in powder or fine ground form, it is more digestible than the whole seeds.

GUAR GUM

Derived from the seed of a legume, guar gum has many times the thickening power of cornflower. Using too much can produce a heavy or stringy texture, so weigh it carefully.

GRAM OR CHICKPEA FLOUR

Gram, or chickpea flour, is also known as besan. The flour is pale yellow, ground from whole chickpeas and contains high protein and fibre. Like other bean flours, gram flour is characterised by a distinct earthy flavour you may not like in large quantities. Best for savoury recipes or in a blend of flours for something like gingerbread or muffins.

MAIZE FLOUR

See also polenta and cornmeal. Maize is a cereal grain. The seed kernels are used to produce light flour that is golden in colour and sweet flavoured. In baking, the grind makes a difference: a coarse grind (like polenta) will give a different texture result than a finer flour (maize), or a very light starch (cornflour). All are useful to blend for gluten-free flour.

MILLET FLOUR

The flour of the millet seed is a creamy off-white colour and the flavour is mild.

NUT FLOURS

Look for a fine-milled version of almond flour if adding to a blend for baking. Otherwise, whole or blanched almonds, hazelnuts, etc. tend to be ground more coarsely. A small proportion of ground nuts added to chocolate cakes and bakes or cheesecake bases will lend their background flavour and create a denser, fudgy texture.

Nuts, such as cashews or almonds soaked in a little water and then puréed, will make fabulous, creamy nut milks or thicker 'butters': always a great alternative to dairy for sauces, cakes and cookie dough.

OAT FLOUR

Oats contain a protein, avenin, which is similar to gluten and so may not be suitable for all people with coeliac disease. The source of oats must be certified gluten free to avoid contamination by other grains during processing.

Oats are packed with nutrition, and adding a little oat flour to your blend can make a softer crumb in cakes and bread. Try it in carrot cake, muffins and soda bread. Look out for the different grain sizes from coarse to fine.

Oat milk is a great alternative for dairy free, but commercial cartons often contain gluten.

POTATO FLOUR AND POTATO STARCH

Potato starch is a pure white, very light, fine starch powder, with a neutral flavour. It is ground from the dehydrated starch of potatoes (rather than from the whole potato as with potato flour). Potato starch will help to give a light and airy texture to baked products.

Potato starch should not be confused with potato flour, which is a different product. Potato flour can be made from cooked potatoes, dried and ground, or processed from dried raw potato.

As you might expect, potato flour has a distinctive potato flavour and a heavy texture. A little goes a long way.

QUINOA

Quinoa is a seed. It adds valuable nutrition, is easily digestible and is gluten free. The fine ground flour has a heavier texture and a distinctive earthy taste, so it's advisable to use sparingly and blended with other flours. It is great to use in baked recipes with chocolate or bold flavours. In salads, etc. rinse and drain the wholegrains well before using.

SORGHUM FLOUR

Sorghum is from the grass family, the whole grain is milled to a light tan-coloured flour; it has a subtle flavour and texture, similar to wheat. Sorghum softens, with a slight sweetness

and also gives good results when combined with millet and gluten-free oat flours, for an alternative gluten-free flour blend.

Sorghum flour can be substituted for brown rice flour for a finer texture. It's not suitable for delicate paler cakes, but it is higher in protein and fibre than brown rice flour. Other names include jowar flour and cholam, and it is widely known in India and Africa.

SOYA FLOUR

Soya flour is a high-protein flour. It is best combined with other flours to form an alternative to wheat flour. It can be good in breads, as the protein helps to produce a good structure, but it is best used in small amounts and combined with other, softer flours to tenderise the crumb.

TEFF FLOUR

Teff flour is from an ancient grain and has a bold, slightly sweet and malty flavour. It has some gelling properties, so can be useful to hold gluten-free goods together. Teff produces creamy brown wholegrain flour, and can enrich the nutritional quality of recipes.

TAPIOCA FLOUR OR STARCH

Tapioca produces a fine, light and velvety flour, made from the starch extracted from the cassava root (also called manioc). Tapioca helps bind gluten-free recipes and adds crispness to crusts. Sometimes, baked goods lack the mouthfeel you get from wheat flour, and tapioca can bring a useful 'chew' to the texture. It can bake a little tough, so blend with a softer starch like potato flour or cornflour.

XANTHAN GUM

Xanthan is a natural gum made by fermenting corn sugar with friendly bacteria. The bacterium used is Xanthomonas campestris, hence the name xanthan gum.

When added to gluten-free flour mixes, xanthan gum helps to replace the gluten 'stretch factor' and is used like a thickening agent.

Using too much will produce a heavy, gummy texture, so weigh it carefully. It needs to be combined with your gluten-free flour mix before adding any liquid.

index

acknowledgements

'Well as always there are a number of people to thank and in no specific order, John Rush & Luigi Bonomi, as always keep everybody on the straight and narrow. Coeliac UK for all the help and continual guidance as everything on the GF world is constantly changing.

Kyle for continued faith, Judith (even though she is an Arsenal supporter) for keeping John & Luigi in place. Photographer Kate Whitaker for stunning shots, great food styling from Annie Rigg, props Liz Belton and Lydia Brun. Big thanks to copy-editor: Caroline McArthur, prooofreader Corinne Masciocchi and editorial assistant Hannah Coughlin for interpreting my scribble and being extremely patient.

Bea Harling for all the help, I really couldn't do it without you! Your knowledge and meticulous attention to detail, you are the best. Jonny McWilliams my new agent, thanks for taking over and If I've left anyone out I apologise, it wasn't intended.

To you all a big thank you.

Phil'

Bea Harling is an experienced food writer, recipe developer and food scientist working with Phil for many years. Bea also tutors cookery workshops in allergen free baking and cooking.